DATE DUE

CONSUMER-CENTRIC
HEALTHCARE

Opportunities and Challenges for Providers

CONSUMER-CENTRIC HEALTHCARE

Opportunities and Challenges for Providers

Colin B. Konschak
and
Lindsey P. Jarrell

ACHE Management Series

Your board, staff, or clients may also benefit from this book's insight. For more information on quantity discounts, contact the Health Administration Press Marketing Manager at (312) 424–9470.

Library of Congress Cataloging-in-Publication Data
Konschak, Colin.
   Consumer-centric healthcare : opportunities and challenges for providers / Colin Konschak and Lindsey Jarrell.
      p. ; cm. — (ACHE management series)
   Includes bibliographical references.
   ISBN 978-1-56793-367-3 (alk. paper)
   1. Medical care—United States—Marketing. 2. Preferred provider organizations (Medical care)—United States—Marketing. 3. Health maintenance organizations—United States—Marketing. 4. Patient satisfaction—United States. I. Jarrell, Lindsey. II. Title. III. Series: Management series (Ann Arbor, Mich.)
   [DNLM: 1. Delivery of Health Care—organization & administration—United States. 2. Consumer Participation—United States. 3. Marketing of Health Services—United States. 4. Patient Satisfaction—United States. W 84 AA1]
   RA410.56.K66 2010
   362.1068'8—dc22

                              2010036574

The paper used in this publication meets the minimum requirements of American National Standard for Information Sciences—Permanence of Paper for Printed Library Materials, ANSI Z39.48-1984. ♾ ™

Acquisitions editor: Eileen Lynch; Project manager: Samantha Raue; Cover designer: Scott Miller; Cover illustrator: Sean Kane; Layout: BookComp

Found an error or a typo? We want to know! Please e-mail it to hap1@ache.org, and put "Book Error" in the subject line.

For photocopying and copyright information, please contact Copyright Clearance Center at www.copyright.com or at (978) 750–8400.

Health Administration Press
A division of the Foundation of the American
   College of Healthcare Executives
One North Franklin Street, Suite 1700
Chicago, IL 60606–3529
(312) 424–2800

Contents

Detailed Contents

Acknowledgments

WE WOULD LIKE TO THANK our wives, Dr. Millie Lee and Jacqueline Jarrell, for giving us the time and space to write this book and for their ever-present love and support. Thanks also to our clients for giving us the opportunity to confirm our observations and test our ideas with some of the best and the brightest healthcare executives and administrators in the industry.

We would also like to thank Eileen Lynch, our acquisitions editor, whose enthusiasm for the project made it a reality, and Samantha Raue, our project manager, for bringing this book across the finish line.

Introduction

THE DEMOCRATIZATION OF INFORMATION, intensifying as more people gain broadband connection to the Internet, is turning the healthcare field on its head. From the time the first elder dispensed treatment to a tribe member until the Internet age, the model of care essentially remained intact. A knowledgeable, seemingly omnipotent provider used his experience, observation, and magic to aid those in need. They came to him with gashes from saber-toothed tigers, bad cramps from eating the wrong kinds of berries, and complications from childbirth. Healers, who would one day be called doctors, wielded an enormous power over others, and much of that power was psychological in nature.

In his 1979 book *The Psychological Society*, Martin L. Gross explains how even witch doctors, with little authentic medical knowledge, could be highly effective in treating others if the patients believed the witch doctor had healing powers. Many ailments heal themselves, and circumstances, time, and rest account for much of any doctor's so-called success. Through trial, study, and application, healing practitioners developed expert knowledge and established a long-term model for the doctor–patient relationship. The physician's role in society was secure, sacrosanct, and seemingly permanent.

Doctors everywhere were pillars of their communities. In capitalist societies, they were more likely to be prosperous than other citizens. The general practitioner was known by all, respected by most, revered by some, and heeded by whoever wanted to get or remain healthy.

Specialists who rose to the top of their disciplines were particularly prosperous, beyond the grasp of ordinary citizens. They served as the exalted gatekeepers of extraordinarily critical information: how to heal the body after it had come under attack, been injured, been subjected to contagion, or otherwise ceased to function properly.

THE DISTRIBUTION OF INFORMATION POWER

The rise of the personal computer began in 1981. Internet connectivity reached a critical mass in the mid 1990s and yielded information power the ordinary consumer had never before experienced.

Search engines give users information power at their fingertips, and health endures as a popular search topic. People go online to gather information about diet, nutrition, illness, injury, and surgery. They seek answers about symptoms, conditions, treatments, and options.

Today's healthcare patient is more a consumer than a patient. He has greater control over the decisions that affect his healthcare than anyone could have predicted a few decades ago. The average consumer enjoys ultra-easy access to general health information and demands access to his medical records. He expects to open his laptop or check his smartphone and gain instant, unencumbered information access, every hour of every day.

Even people who are not so conncected have elevated healthcare expectations. For hospitals in particular, this unprecedented wave of consumerism is a disruptive force. The best providers adopt effective operational strategies that address consumerism, while providers who ignore consumerism risk becoming irrelevant and losing customers.

CONSUMERS ARE LEADING THE WAY

In their 2006 book *Redefining Healthcare*, Michael Porter and Elizabeth Olmsted Teisberg identify six basic areas in which consumers have taken control or at least assume some responsibility for aspects of their own healthcare:

1. Consumers actively manage their personal healthcare. They make new lifestyle choices, participate in disease management and prevention, seek out routine care, follow prescribed treatments, and submit to testing when appropriate.
2. Consumers seek appropriate information concerning their health needs and research provider results related to specific medical conditions. They seek help interpreting the information they receive from doctors and health insurers, and they are not shy about using independent medical information sources when needed.
3. Consumers make treatment and provider choices that are consistent with their personal values. They base their choices on anticipated results, not on personal convenience or provider amenities, and on perceived quality, not on proximity or past relationships.
4. Consumers choose health plans that offer value-added benefits and features, and they expect health plans to address an array of potential health issues. They choose cost-effective health plan structures that include health savings accounts.
5. Consumers seek long-term participation in their health plan and have little desire to switch to a new insurer unless factors are compelling.
6. Consumers are more likely now than ever to act responsibly about their health and healthcare, detailing their organ donorship and end-of-life care intentions, designating healthcare proxies, and preparing living wills.

Customers can be finicky, and their desires are prompting dramatic changes in how providers deliver healthcare. The rising wave of consumerism is shifting the fundamental balance of economics within healthcare just as consumerism has made an impact on every other industry, and the effects are permanent. The traditional supply-driven economic model is falling away as we transition to a demand-driven system. This new system is characterized by consumer demand for services based on price, quality, and ease of access.

Quality Is Elusive

The unwary provider who does not understand that consumers expect high quality is at a competitive disadvantage. Quality is no longer a feature providers can tout to differentiate themselves from competitors; to consumers, it is a given. Taking quality off the table creates challenges for the provider that has labored diligently for decades to differentiate itself on the basis of quality.

Quality Is in the Eye of the End User

Quality ultimately is defined by and, more important, perceived by the end user. The end user—the consumer—has a different notion of what is an effective mix in the delivery of services and care.

Word of mouth can be invaluable in gaining more customers. Some hospitals capture a sizable share of their target market because they pay attention to consumer concerns and frequently demonstrate that they are responsive to needs, and consumers share their satisfaction with others.

If a particular provider does not meet their needs, consumers find an alternative solution that better meets their expectations. They vote with their dollars. The younger the consumer—especially those in generations X and Y—the more likely she is to explore innovative ways of receiving healthcare services. But generational differences pale in comparison to the overall, across-the-board shifts in consumers' approaches to healthcare.

All consumers seek greater convenience, and many are willing to pay for it. Surveys show most consumers are interested in the availability of same-day appointments. About two out of three understand the importance and value of wellness programs. More than three out of five seek tools that offer personalized health recommendations, and nearly equal numbers want tools for assessing, managing, and monitoring their health (Deloitte 2008).

People are becoming more sophisticated and savvy about healthcare issues, their own healthcare, and the resources available to them. They are looking for trusted partners to whom they will offer their long-term allegiance. The welcome news about the healthcare consumerism revolution is that healthcare needs are not going away; needs will increase as people live longer, desire a better quality of life, and continually seek out providers who can help them to do so.

Even in turbulent economic times needs don't disappear. They shift. Those who understand the nature of the shifts are best able to benefit from them. We begin with a discussion of the transparent provider in which we focus on how you and your hospital can come to be regarded as the default healthcare provider to your target market.

CHAPTER 1

The Transparent Provider

IN THIS CHAPTER:

- Consumers want specifics
- The transition to transparency
- Perception equals quality
- What is your health grade?

IN HIS 1963 ESSAY "Uncertainty and the Welfare Economics of Medical Care" in the *American Economic Review*, author Kenneth J. Arrow depicts the healthcare market as one of imperfect competition due to pervasive uncertainties in the marketplace, asymmetric information, and the lack of markets for selected healthcare procedures or services.

In years past healthcare was driven by providers and insurers with little input from the actual end user: the patient. The demand for enhanced healthcare has increased as healthcare information becomes more widely available. Consumerism is a major development poised to profoundly and irrevocably have an impact on all healthcare-field stakeholders.

ARMED WITH FACTS, AND TAKING CHARGE

In the report "Marketing in Times of Price Transparency," Carolyn Kent, creative strategy specialist at the hospital financial strength services organization Cleverley + Associates, contends that providers today must be prepared to talk price. "The reality is that people are going to continue to ask about it, whether they be consumers, media personnel, or another interested party. The hospitals that are making a visible attempt to engage in an open dialogue about price transparency, the hospitals that are not afraid to discuss their pricing structure with the media, are going to gain the public's trust and position themselves as industry thought leaders" (2007, 2–3).

A growing percentage of consumers are committed activists for their healthcare. They evaluate price and quality information, select vendors, and patronize alternative healthcare services. Even more consumers seek to become healthcare activists. Empowered by technology, increasingly they seek access to comparison data that enable them to make healthcare decisions with more confidence.

By any analysis, we have entered an age where, aided by the Internet, people are more predisposed to take charge of various aspects of their careers and domestic lives than ever before. Americans are exhibiting more interest in the availability, quality, and cost of healthcare services than the field traditionally has been accustomed to.

Individuals today readily do the groundwork to understand the health challenges they face and what their options are for resolution. Armed with the ability to compare costs between providers, they do so eagerly. They want to know why a certain test or procedure has been recommended instead of an alternate option.

Today's healthcare consumers are willing to explore alternative care options such as the ancient Chinese practice of acupuncture, which is growing in popularity in the United States and is often covered under health plans. They consider seeing chiropractors, dietitians and nutritional specialists, and naturopaths if they believe significant health benefits will accrue.

Perhaps the most intriguing aspect of this new wave of consumerism is that consumers readily seek out the opinions of fellow consumers on websites, blogs, chat rooms, and forums that give them perspectives about specific providers and treatments—information that was simply unavailable to previous generations of healthcare consumers.

From Out of the Darkness

From the 1950s until the Internet age, the healthcare field propagated a system in which there could be dozens or even hundreds of different prices for the same medical procedure. Because the healthcare consumer was not privy to any cost or outcome analyses, he made decisions based on the provider's proximity or general reputation, newspaper or magazine articles, and word-of-mouth recommendations from friends and family.

The enormous popularity of the Internet, the rise of search engines, the appearance of aggregator sites offering cost and quality comparison information, the federal government's call for transparency in the healthcare field, and a weak economy all contribute to a burgeoning mass of vigilant consumers who want answers from the healthcare field just as they want answers from the other industries they patronize.

In a few short years, the healthcare field—hospitals in particular—has been forced to embrace a new model for the delivery of medical services. This model is driven by consumers, supported at the highest levels of government, and facilitated by an electronic highway that grows in strength each day as a source of reliable cost and comparison information. As this new, bold, consumer-driven field takes shape, its executives are grappling with the notion that consumers' wants, needs, preferences, and perceptions are fast becoming its guiding forces.

The New Sacrament

Listening to consumers, ministering to their needs, making them feel comfortable, and, most important, addressing how they perceive the quality and services rendered in your hospital has now become sacrosanct. Cold and clinical hospital rooms, waiting rooms, and hallways are giving way to more nurturing environments designed to instill calmness and serenity. Consumers want providers who get the job done and make them feel comfortable in the process.

The hospital that succeeds in the coming decade will be the one that masters creating a sense of partnership with consumers, helping them contain costs, working with them to maintain or improve their health, and demonstrating through a variety of factors that there is no reason for consumers to take their business anywhere else.

Carolyn Kent (2006) points out that many providers are already offering classes to the general public on preventive care measures. Kent suggests offering classes about what to expect during a stay, how to understand a hospital bill, and how to be a more informed healthcare consumer. While there are obstacles to making price information widely available, providers need to understand that customers demand transparency and want to talk price. Perhaps the single most effective way to reinforce this message is to become a transparent provider—one that meets federal mandates of transparency and matches the competition in price, quality, and other core measures that a prudent consumer would want to know, while offering up-to-the-minute information via a website so navigable that anyone could visit and find what she needs with minimal effort.

Employers and insurers are at the helm in advancing the movement toward industry transparency. A few providers have voluntarily made public their quality and price information. Soon all providers will do so, either because they are federally mandated to or because industry standards will rise such that transparency cannot be ignored.

Often a handful of local employers account for a significant portion of a hospital's patient population. If that is the case at your facility, to what degree are you supporting employers who seek to offer their employees a single contact point where they can quickly and easily track their experiences? Does your hospital offer simple tools for identifying the best local care at the most attractive cost?

Implications for Your Hospital

A growing number of consumers seek, or will be seeking, comprehensive consumer data about providers, which means that industry-wide transparency is inevitable. As more consumers seek the ability to make good choices about their healthcare, you must address these issues:

- When will your hospital adopt a culture of transparency?
- Are you exploring what industry leaders are doing?
- Have you appointed staff to lead this crucial aspect of operations?
- In addition to standard reporting measures, are there unique ways to highlight your strengths?
- If you were a consumer considering your own hospital, what information would you like to have readily available before making a decision?
- Do you offer free consumer classes about pricing or plan to do so?
- What other transparency-related outreach efforts could be appropriate for you?

SECRECY DOESN'T SELL

Hospitals traditionally have practiced some secrecy regarding survey results to avoid patient dissatisfaction and potential lawsuits. Surveys have confirmed most hospital administrators prefer to shun transparency, avoid reporting medical errors, and conduct business as usual (Weissman et al. 2005). In states where mandatory public disclosure is already in effect, however, patient dissatisfaction and lawsuits have not increased, and the urge for secrecy among hospital executives and administrators dissipated soon after the public disclosure rules came into effect.

When a provider makes results available, the risk of lawsuits can actually decline, because a more informed patient understands the true risk in any procedure and is less likely to litigate for malpractice if something does go wrong. Today's consumers are not ignorant. They know that airplanes crash, government officials are sometimes corrupt, and hospitals sometimes lose patients as a result of faulty diagnoses, wrong medications, or other human error.

Providers who hold themselves accountable and publicly disclose less-than-stellar results gain admiration from the surrounding hospital community. In other words, as scary as transparency may seem at the outset, the experience of those who have become transparent has been something altogether different.

Transparency Breeds Confidence

The transparent provider displays an unyielding commitment to quality, to the patient experience, and most important, to patient outcomes. Transparency signals that a provider strives for excellence and is dedicated to overall improvement. Moreover, as a provider begins to identify, collect, and prepare the data from core measures, the willingness to disseminate that information increases.

The founder of the Institute for Healthcare Improvement, Donald Berwick, has observed that providing patients with quality, price, and comparison information sets the stage for the provider to make a true and lasting commitment to excellence. The sooner such reports are collected and disseminated, the quicker the provider's reputation can be enhanced.

For example, the Cleveland Clinic, based in Cleveland, Ohio, has enjoyed a decades-long reputation for excellent patient care.

The clinic first published its clinical outcomes and experience in thoracic and cardiac surgery in an annual report in 1999. After five years the reporting was expanded to include some other practice units. Today every practice unit and clinical department at the clinic is required to establish and publish its vital outcome data.

Aggregate data from providers everywhere is also becoming readily available on the Internet. Following are just two examples—one from government and one from the private sector—of the enormousness of the data available. And this is just the beginning.

Medicare's Hospital Compare

Medicare's Hospital Compare (www.hospitalcompare.hhs.gov) is a public and private collaboration created to help promote public disclosure of the quality of care offered by hospitals. Hospital Compare is supported by the Hospital Quality Alliance (HQA), which consists of a variety of organizations, such as the AARP, the American Hospital Association, the American Nurses Association, and the U.S. Chamber of Commerce, among others, who collectively represent hospitals, doctors and nurses, federal agencies, employers, accrediting agencies, and, of course, consumers.

Hospital Compare is available for any consumer who wants to obtain reliable information on providers. The site indicates whether a provider offers the recommended care for patients with conditions such as pneumonia, heart attack, heart failure, and childhood asthma, or for patients having surgery. The site also displays rates for the process-of-care measures.

Providers voluntarily provide their own data from the records they keep. The data submitted include patients who have Medicare, those who are enrolled in a Medicare health plan, and those who do not have Medicare.

Hospital Compare displays data on 30-day risk-adjusted mortality, readmission rates, the number of Medicare patients treated, inpatient hospital payment information, and the volume of Medicare patients treated by specific illness or diagnosis. Currently, psychiatric, rehabilitation, and long-term-care hospitals and their operating data are not reported on the website.

The data offered on Hospital Compare indicates how well a hospital is able to care for its patients, but as the site notes, small differences in percentages usually don't mean much. Also, scores may be affected by how many patients are included in the calculations.

HealthGrades

HealthGrades (www.healthgrades.com), an independent healthcare ratings organization, issues reports and ratings on 5,000 hospitals, 16,000 nursing homes, and 750,000 physicians to help site visitors identify quality care providers. Users can search in several ways. They can select a procedure or diagnosis such as carotid surgery, heart bypass surgery, bowel obstruction, or respiratory failure, and from there they can see which hospitals and which doctors provide services. Visitors can also select one of HealthGrades' many award recipient categories, such as America's 50 Best Hospitals, hospitals distinguished for clinical excellence, hospitals noted for outstanding patient experience, and hospitals receiving patient safety or specialty excellence awards.

HealthGrades is constantly updating its information to keep visitors informed. It also provides services to specific users, such as the HealthGrades Connecting Point, which matches patients to a provider's doctors; the Clinical Excellence Research and Consulting group, which connects providers with HealthGrades' physician-led team of expert consultants to improve quality; and HealthGrades ratings and awards, where providers can partner with HealthGrades to enhance their reputation among patients, employers, and the general public.

HealthGrades offers medical-cost reports to help users spend their healthcare dollars wisely and better plan for future healthcare expenditures. The site offers reports on bunion correction, bone marrow biopsy, hernia repair, liver biopsy, tubal ligation, pacemaker implant, and ear tube placement, among dozens of other procedures. Users can also get cost reports based on a range of visit types, such as dermatology, emergency room, gynecology, oncology, and reproductive medicine.

A Watchdog for Unnecessary Procedures

Missing from much of the transparency information being generated for public consumption is an objective analysis of whether particular procedures are medically justified. *Consumer Reports* (2005) suggests that these 12 operations are performed more often than they may actually be needed:

- Angiography
- Angioplasty
- Back-pain procedures
- Cesarean section
- Circumcision
- Enlarged-prostate procedures
- Episiotomy
- Heartburn procedures
- Hysterectomy
- Prostatectomy
- Weight-loss surgery
- Wisdom-tooth extraction

TAKE A LEADING ROLE

Making the decision to take the lead as a transparent provider is a huge step, and it requires careful planning and concern. Alegent Health, a faith-based healthcare network located throughout Nebraska and southwestern Iowa, has 10 hospitals, more than 100 service sites, 1,300 doctors, and a combined workforce of 9,000. Alegent's quest for transparency began in 2005 following the decision to publicize its patient-care quality scores.

In September 2005 the hospital placed a full-page advertisement in the local newspaper, presenting data on its performance in the care of pneumonia, heart attacks, and heart failure. Employing a composite scoring methodology, Alegent presented the performance of each of its ten hospitals as well as its overall system scores and compared its results to the regional average for hospitals based on data from the Centers for Medicare & Medicaid Services. Alegent hospitals did not rank highest in every category, which surprised its doctors and employees. It took courage to make such scores public. The executive staff and board of directors believed it was the correct course of action and demonstrated a clear commitment to the long-term embrace of transparency: after all, it would be easy to publish scores if they were all superlative. One of Alegent's scores was actually below the regional average (Sensor 2009).

Enroll the Staff

Recognizing that doctors and other employees would need to be part of the process, Alegent held a series of dialogues with them to explore the new paradigm, address concerns, and listen to questions. As the doctors and staff accepted the fact that Alegent was committed to transparency and organizational transformation, good things started to happen. Medical and administrative staff on all levels felt empowered to offer recommendations for improving scores. Lingering concerns about Alegent's embrace of transparency disappeared as the staff realized improvements in quality were occurring regularly.

Alegent began to share with employees advance copies of newspaper ads featuring its scores. Before long, nearly everyone employed in the system assumed the mantle of stakeholder. The quality scores continued to rise, and in 2008, Alegent Health was cited by the Network for Regional Healthcare Improvement as the nation's number-one health system.

Today, Alegent voluntarily publishes reports on 40 different quality scores, 21 of which indicate how often Alegent's hospitals offered recommended care for pneumonia, heart attack, and heart failure. Another nine factors, developed by the Surgical Care Improvement Project (SCIP), a national partnership of organizations, focus on improving surgical care.

SENSITIVITY ABOUT PRICE INFORMATION

What one hospital charges for a particular procedure varies widely based on a host of factors. Understandably, many providers who are otherwise enthusiastic about transparency about patient outcomes are reticent to disclose cost data. There are real reasons for concern, as we shall discuss in Chapter 7 on the globalization of medicine. But there also are compelling reasons for being transparent with prices. For one, today's consumers are armed with price information that exceeds anything they could have assembled even a few years earlier. Consumers have access to so much price information in their everyday lives, they expect it from healthcare services too. Second, in the mind of many consumers, price equals quality.

To take an example from another industry: wine sold under one label is sometimes deemed more valuable than wine under another label, even if the wine itself is exactly the same.

Reputation Enhances Price

At the supermarket, branded merchandise still sells at a higher price than generic brands with the same ingredients. Similarly, your hospital's reputation could help persuade a patient to pay more to be treated by you over others who offer the same care and service.

Suppose a consumer does his homework and finds that you and a competitor have entirely equal success rates for a particular procedure but you charge 15 percent more. Is this a reason to fear price transparency? No, because with all the data available for a consumer to peruse, the decision to choose one provider over another is multifaceted. Price is one factor, albeit an important one, among several.

So You Want Cost Data

At Alegent Health, the prevailing attitude is that consumers have a right to know how much a provider charges (Sensor 2009). In January 2007, Alegent launched My Cost (www.alegent.com/mycost), a consumer-friendly feature that offers cost estimates for a variety of tests, procedures, appointments, and services.

Visitors can simply enter the name of their insurance provider, select the treatment, and provide copayment or deductible information. The system then presents a cost estimate. The visitor is also treated to financial assistance information via links. In the first three years of its existence, more than 50,000 cost estimates were generated through My Cost.

Alegent's experience in promoting price transparency has been that consumers appreciate the honesty and openness of the organization. Instead of price transparency scaring away potential business, in this case it has led to stronger provider–patient relationships. Former Alegent CEO Wayne Sensor says price and quality transparency "isn't necessarily easy, and it does take courage, but in the end it is the right thing to do for consumers and the community" (Sensor 2009).

MAKE THE COMMITMENT

Commitment to transparency takes bravery. But what other choice is there? Fortunately, as we will see, there is room for creativity and initiative.

It is imperative you provide information about your hospital's results as to medical condition outcomes. Your data need to include (1) patient outcomes with an adjustment for risk based on prior conditions, (2) the overall cost of care, and (3) measurements for both extending through the care cycle. Transparency also encompasses offering the experience your hospital has in treating specific medical conditions by volume of patients, delineated by methods of care.

Some website restructuring—such as adding a large, highly inviting consumer section—can aid in cost transparency. Be proactive and invite the consumer to comb through your data. Just as industrial companies publish annual reports with profit and loss statements, balance sheets, and cash flow analyses, you might choose to offer a five-year projection of the life cycle cost of a procedure and its follow-up.

Details Count

Outcomes for a specific medical condition can and should be expressed many ways. For example, in shoulder surgery several validated measures exist, such as range of movement, reduction of pain, and ability to function. Still other outcome measures for shoulder surgery include the interval between the initiation of care and return to normal activity, such as returning to work or playing tennis again.

Data related to the particulars of patients—known as patient attributes—such as gender, age, genetic factors, and prevailing conditions, are critical elements of transparency and are essential for assessing risk. A transparent provider also publishes measures of diagnostic accuracy, including cost, timeliness, and completeness. Outcome measures that only address episodic interventions fall short because they fail to yield results meaningful to the patient. Such shortsighted reporting and consequence scoring can be counterproductive and lead to the publication of misleading data.

Failure is unpleasant, and people, much like organizations, instinctively want to avoid reporting their own shortcomings. Still, ineffective treatments—errors in procedure, medication, or treatment—and complications following a procedure need to be identified and scored. As difficult as this task may be, it is a step on the path to improved treatment and overall service. You cannot fix a problem you refuse to acknowledge.

Expand Your Measures

You may be able to devise your own data measures by building on traditional data measures. For example, you could align your total quality management efforts, such as your Six Sigma Performance Improvement initiatives, around improving the 30-day readmission rate. You may wish to devise multiple strategies to improve the scores on each of the core measures that need to be fully transparent. Rest assured other providers will do the same.

Cost Mysteries No More

Unlike most businesses, many hospitals don't know what their actual charges ought to be. They charge based on tradition, competition, payer contracts, or whatever cost data they can scrape together. A comprehensive understanding of true cost is often lacking. If the government mandates that hospitals publish price and quality information, hospitals will need the technical ability to do so.

Implications for Your Hospital

Is transparency part of your agenda for your weekly and monthly meetings?

- Has your hospital developed policies and procedures in relation to transparency?
- Within your own office or division, are top officers involved in the transparency discussion?
- Have you attended any conferences or symposiums about transparency?
- Are you monitoring other providers who have already made the conversion to transparency?
- Are you devising plans to capitalize on the inherent opportunities in offering transparent data?

THE PATIENT ABOVE ALL ELSE

To understand the actual value of the services you render to patients, you have to maintain a long-term relationship with them. This means periodically making contact to monitor how they're doing, how they feel, what has transpired since the last contact, what new needs they may have, and what has worked best for them. It is costly to develop and maintain such patient registries, but the continuing display of care and concern for the patients and the development of longer-term relationships can lead to increased business. After appropriate systems are in place, such monitoring can be done with less effort and lower cost. Information from other parties who serve the patient, such as medical device suppliers, drugstores, and health service firms, can add to the scope of your data.

Patient feedback is a vital tool in the quest for transparency and in improving the overall quality and perceived value of your services. The patient's experience of ease of appointment-making, waiting time, access to the doctor, attention to individual needs, amenities, discharge procedures, and follow-up are all valuable inputs that are overruled perhaps only by the patient's ultimate perception of the quality and the outcome of her medical procedure.

Observe the Leaders, but Chart Your Own Path

Because many leading providers across the nation are already making core measures transparent, you have the opportunity to see, and improve on, what the leaders are offering. The more transparency measures you encounter in your study, the greater the opportunity you have to align the mix of measures in your transparency efforts.

You may want to include some nontraditional measures. For example, a savvy consumer might want to know, "Does the hospital have an automated system that checks for drug interactions when administering medications?"

Manage Perception

To consumers, perception is everything. If they feel like they're being treated well and looked after, your organization will benefit. Conversely, if consumers are being treated well but perceive that they aren't, they will feel agitated. Hospitals have to treat the patient well and manage the perception that they are doing so. Ultimately patients' views can be reflected in the transparency data you generate.

You can increase perceived value in other small ways. For example, consider handing out a card to patients during their stay that asks, "How are we doing today?" It's a small, inexpensive gesture, but it can have a strong impact on perception.

Give patients the opportunity to log on to your website and make comments about the quality of their stay. Construct a brief survey about their visit, asking questions such as, "Was the desk reception friendly?" As we'll discuss in Chapter 8, through use of social media such as Twitter and Facebook, patients can easily give updates in real time. Someone at your hospital could monitor comments posted on social media, aggregate them, and provide feedback to the executive staff.

Perhaps more important, such feedback could help the floor staff improve care. From these real-time comments, you could glean information such as whether a particular patient would prefer to have the newspaper delivered first thing each day. With some ingenuity you could create patient satisfaction scores that could be compiled and included in your transparency efforts.

Learn from Other Industries

W hotels offer a signature concierge service called Whatever/Whenever. Just as it sounds, the service offers guests whatever they want, whenever they want it—custom room service, restaurant reservations, technical assistance, and other conveniences, for a sliding-scale fee.

Small personal touches can make a difference, as can literal touches. A Tampa Bay–area hospital has initiated a new process—if a nurse or allied health professional is about to leave a patient's room, he has to turn, actually touch the patient (if conditions allow), and say, "Is there anything else I might do for you before I leave?" This process has led to a notable rise in patient satisfaction scores. Patients who experienced the touch rated the quality of care higher than did patients who had not received the touch, even when no other discernable measures of quality were provided.

The key in touching the patient is to offer an authentic person-to-person gesture that is warm and friendly and given with the complete intention to serve.

Doctors Can Work Miracles

Your doctors can go a long way in enhancing perceived quality. If a doctor enters a room and sits down with the patient for ten seconds or so, no matter what else happens, the patient perceives that the doctor cares.

Suppose the doctor walks in, never sits down, and leaves. No matter how attentive and caring the doctor may be in reality, the patient may perceive that she is unworthy of the doctor's attention.

Implications for Your Hospital

Have you implemented a campaign to identify all areas of perception management?

- Are you surveying patients or otherwise providing outlets for their expression?
- What possible measures are emerging as a result of your exploration?
- Are there guidelines for doctors, nurses, and medical staff for offering an added personal touch?
- How do you support these efforts by rewarding employees who capitulate and correcting those who do not?
- Are you developing other strategies for delighting patients?

TRANSPARENCY AS A TOOL OF DISTINCTION

The transparent provider of the near future will:

- make research data available for the consumer;
- exceed all requirements for reporting and compiling data; and

- share up-front information about costs, procedures, long-term and recent experience in certain areas, doctors' and medical staff's background and unique experience and capabilities, and the experiences of other consumers.

Such boldness aids in establishing local or regional dominance, being ahead of the field, and becoming the default provider for the target market. This may require a redesign of your website, or adding new links to your existing website that enable consumers to quickly find what they're seeking.

HOT TIPS AND INSIGHTS

- Consumers who seek comprehensive price and quality compel providers to embrace transparency.
- Providers who hold themselves accountable and publicly disclose all results tend to gain admiration.
- Making the commitment to transparency is a huge, inevitable step, but one that can encompass creativity and initiative and help build business.
- To consumers, perception is everything, and the wise provider helps to influence such perceptions through extraordinary attentiveness.
- The transparent provider offers comprehensive, consumer-friendly research data above and beyond any reporting requirements.

CHAPTER 2

Information Technology Goes Mobile

IN THIS CHAPTER:

- The promise of information technology
- The ubiquitous smartphone
- Who gets to define quality?
- E-patients and their impact

HOSPITALS HAVE EMPLOYED information technology since the early days of mainframe computers. Unlike previous eras, however, the marriage of information technology (IT) and personal portable technology today is redefining the hospital–patient relationship and determining which hospitals will flourish in the upcoming decade.

The United States on the whole hasn't experienced any healthcare cost containment since 1997. White House officials have proclaimed that IT in healthcare is the key to containing costs in the future, and with sufficient reason: effective use of health IT helps to increase productivity through data mining, medical data warehousing, reduction of medical errors, and avoidance of inappropriate or redundant care. The administration has likened the development of comprehensive healthcare IT to grand, national investments of the past including the interstate highway system and the electrification of rural areas, both of which increased aggregate productivity and the gross domestic product.

Let's examine the coming shift to full IT adoption from the perspectives of hospitals, doctors, and patients.

THE TOOL OF THE CENTURY

IT in hospitals is a key tool that can help provide smoother operations and a higher level of healthcare. An effective IT system enables a provider to efficiently collect, compile, and apply patient information on prognoses, activities, therapies, costs, and outcomes for each encounter, over time, for the complete cycle of care. It enables providers to abandon the old framework of healthcare as episodic, discrete interventions and embrace a full-spectrum approach to individual healthcare. IT facilitates the delivery of healthcare through integrated medical teams and therapies that can result in vastly upgraded healthcare. This potential has tantalized the field for more than a decade; now it is time to put the technology into practice.

Breaking Cost Barriers

The cost of establishing and installing an IT system has been a barrier for many hospitals. This barrier was especially difficult in the days when system features proved too expensive for the value they provided. The benefits of IT are becoming clearer, but underinvestment still plagues many providers. Per-staff-person investment in healthcare IT trails that of private industry by 100 to 400 percent: $3,000 is spent per person, on average, versus a range of $7,000 to $15,000 per person in other industries (Porter and Teisberg 2006, 213).

The forces of the federal government, progressive competitors, and an increasingly demanding populace will surely bring healthcare IT investment more in line with that in other industries. However, the initiatives, programs, services, maintenance, and task forces required to get healthcare IT up to speed will require a gargantuan effort. And once IT is in place, it is not a cure-all. It is a tool—albeit a huge, multifaceted, complex one—and as with all tools, it works best in the hands of able users.

The Patient Is the Focus

At the heart of any IT system is the patient, the basic unit around which essential data are assembled, stored, and retrieved as needed. The patient—not the department, specialty unit, physician, or cost center—determines how an effective IT system is designed.

Personal health records, including appointment history, treatment history, test results, imaging, and billing, are the system's pillars. Such records support an integrated approach to data that works across locations, departments, physicians, and treatments. With such records in place, lower costs can be achieved at virtually every juncture, treatment, and process, and for the overall cycle of care (Porter and Teisberg 2006, 214). (Personal health records will be discussed further in Chapter 3.)

When electronic medical records are established, a plethora of health and quality of service benefits accrue. The hospital is able to lower administrative costs and reduce or eliminate paperwork while making patient information readily available to doctors and nurses. The system supports information-sharing between departments, doctors, and even institutions in real time. Such up-to-date information helps to improve decision-making while reducing duplicate tests and procedures.

A Greater Understanding

Doctors armed with patients' electronic medical records have an immediate and vast potential to better serve the patient, improve patient perception of quality of services, and help to cement longer-term relationships. Fundamentally, the doctor–patient dialogue defines the way in which healthcare is delivered.

Contrast the type of doctor–patient relationship possible through effective use of IT with the all-too-common experience of most patients today: a busy doctor briefly reviews whatever available patient records can be accessed, does her best to offer personalized services, and departs. Later, the patient receives a blizzard of forms, including hard-to-decipher invoices, lab notes, and other impersonal correspondence. Understanding the documents takes effort. Refuting any charges is an ordeal. Effective implementation of IT can prevent this confusion and disorganization.

In Control at the Dashboard

Effective use of IT allows hospitals to provide patients a dashboard that offers them a sense of control. Each user can visit a personalized website and connect to hospital departments, clinics, doctors, and other care providers. Users can make appointments, complete necessary forms online, obtain instructions or logistical information, provide feedback after an appointment or service, obtain test results, get patient education information, and more accurately monitor their healing or recovery programs.

Once a patient connects with the hospital's financial system, he can use his personal dashboard to organize invoices and insurance forms following a hospital visit. The personal page also offers health information customized to the patient and his family, important links, and possible next steps based on treatment outcomes.

The consumer movement's wheels of progress are in motion and there is no turning back. Patients seek and demand the ability to take personal control of their health accounts, just as they are able to do with bank accounts, credit card accounts, and travel arrangements. The patient of the future will assess doctors based in part on the provider's level of IT sophistication.

THE NEW TECH-SAVVY MEDICAL PRACTITIONER

In a 2009 survey of more than 1,000 U.S. medical students, nearly half reported using an iPhone or iPod touch, a Palm, or a Blackberry device. Nearly 60 percent of those who used basic cell phones indicated they planned to purchase a smartphone within the following 12 months (Epocrates 2009). Such IT connectedness is an indicator of the future direction of health services delivery.

Nearly 90 percent of medical students believed health information from online or mobile sources was efficiently credible for daily use and trailed only medical journals as reliable health information sources. Respondents were more than four times more likely to use a mobile health reference in answering a clinical question than to query their attending physician.

Nearly 85 percent of respondents had experience with electronic medical records (EMRs) during their clinical rotation. Ninety percent observed that use of EMRs would be a critical factor in deciding where they would practice medicine (Epocrates 2009). In other words, to attract the best physicians, you need to have IT systems in place.

All doctors today, from first-year residents to 30-year veterans, are affected by the surging tide of health information technology including EMRs, telemedicine, smartphones, and Internet resources. The younger the physician, the more likely she is to embrace the phenomenon, but even many veterans are hooked.

Smartphones Take Over

Smartphones are influencing the way healthcare is delivered. Since Apple began allowing third-party developers to submit applications for the iPhone, healthcare has been swept up in the revolution. The Harvard School of Public Health has developed its own iPhone application, as have many institutions. Harvard's

Swine Flu application explains how to protect against H1N1 and offers updates on the outbreak.

More physicians will adopt health applications, particularly applications related to electronic medical records and clinical decision support. Ultimately health applications result in better healthcare for patients.

From Merely Cool to Essential

The iPhone is increasingly seen as a medical necessity. One mid-Atlantic laparoscopic surgeon who rotates between four hospitals and sees as many as 180 patients in a single week is an iPhone devotee. He uses the device to keep track of patient progress and other details that would otherwise be highly difficult to collect. The iPhone allows him to e-mail billing information back to his office while he is making his rounds. Thus he eliminates paperwork in ways previously unimaginable.

Smartphones can enhance medical care in unprecedented ways. For example, a doctor could take a picture of a strange-looking iris or spots on a leg and immediately send it to a specialist for a second opinion. Or if a patient can't remember what type of medication he is taking, but does recall what the pills look like, the doctor can find pictures of the drug with relative ease and quickly determine the correct medication.

The potential is vast. Because most hospitals have or plan to install Wi-Fi, a new era of technological ease awaits. Integrating a doctor's findings noted on an iPhone into a patient's personal health record and the larger IT system is simple once system-wide protocols and privacy and security measures have been perfected. Doctors want mobile technology for treating patients throughout their days. The question is, can they effectively do so in your facility?

Implications for Your Hospital

Employing external service providers who can seamlessly merge electronic records with facility operations and procedures is one way to provide consumers with services they will come to expect in all hospitals, for all visits. Have you identified external providers who can offer this level of care to your patients?

- How responsive would your patient base be to such services?
- How would it redefine patient perception of the care you provide?
- What are the internal impediments of offering this level of care either through external vendors or internal resources?

TECHNOLOGY IS A TOOL, QUALITY IS THE ISSUE

Hospitals today can harness IT to redefine their relationship with customers and redefine the patient perception of the hospital's quality. The dilemma is that hospital executives invariably believe they understand what quality is and point to an impressive array of clinical indicators and outcomes. Results count, but as highlighted in Chapter 1, what counts far more is how the consumer defines quality. The consumer's perception of quality is likely to differ vastly from that of hospital executives.

How do consumers learn about quality? For many, through their phones. In *The Decision Tree: Taking Control of Your Health in the New Era of Personalized Medicine* (2010), Thomas Goetz claims the next revolution in medicine is happening in consumers' smartphones and personal computers. The explosion of personalized information lets people make better decisions about their own healthcare. Goetz's book, aimed at consumers rather than providers, promises to help readers take control of their own healthcare in "the new era of personalized medicine" and make health choices in an era where the outpouring of medical information has greatly outpaced people's ability to process it.

The options for contacting, staying in touch with, and sending reminders to patients are more diverse and hold more potential than ever before, especially for the provider with IT designed to connect with the personal technology people carry in their pockets. Consumers make treatments and provider choices consistent with their personal values and based on anticipated results. Will the provider's medical expertise be part of the patient's decision-making? Yes and no. The delivery of expert healthcare and service is taken as a given—table stakes you need to have to be in the game.

Quality is always a moving target and defined by the recipient, even if providers wish it were stationary and defined by themselves. Consumers make their choices based on perceived quality, not necessarily on proximity or past relationships. For example, smartphone users tend to centralize information on their phones, using its scheduling capabilities to keep their lives running smoothly. The hospital system that sends tech-savvy patients a text reminder including the appointment time, type, and location confirms in consumers' minds that their healthcare institution is in tune with the times.

It's a simple gesture, but a text or voicemail message about a scheduled appointment conveys to the consumer that the provider understands the patient—or at least the way she schedules her time, arranges her affairs, and runs her life.

Me and My Phone

The consumer who appreciates the text-message appointment reminder also downloads applications for her smartphone, health-related applications among them. The variety of apps your hospital could develop for patients knows no bounds: apps could include the seven tests for cancer, the first signs of a heart attack, how to perform CPR, what to do in case of stroke, how to handle fainting or dizzy spells, or what to do if someone has suffered a concussion.

A good app helps cement in consumers' minds the quality of care your hospital is capable of providing; it shows you are on their wavelength and helps establish you as the go-to source when something is wrong.

Implications for Your Hospital

You can develop apps that accent your strength, be it oncology, OB-GYN, or pediatrics. Does your hospital offer any of these apps?

- Exercise regimens
- Nutrition information
- Guides to help manage specific diseases or chronic conditions
- Medication instructions and compliance assistance

Or none of the above?

Reminders and Amusements

Tech-connected patients want reminder pings—brief timed notifications—asking, for example, "Have you remembered to take your medication today?" These patients might even want pings three times a day, if that's the daily pill regimen. Before the advent of the smartphone, patients were responsible for remembering their medication. But contemporary patients rely on personal technology for help—and this tech reliance cannot be denied or ignored (Ferguson 2007).

Turning to smartphones for instructions, reminders, updates, cues, formulas, and recipes is so ingrained that it's becoming second nature. At the gym, you might see people working with an app offering photos and instructions of that day's exercise routine. At the airport or supermarket, you might witness parents passing their smartphones to their children, offering games to occupy them.

Using IT to meet consumers' demands will likely become a requirement, not just an option, as smartphones grow more powerful and their use more common, a bigger number of better apps becomes available, and life gets more hectic.

Ping to Me

Suppose a ping asks for a patient's response but the response doesn't come. With the right system, someone at the hospital will call and say, "Mr. Williams, you haven't pinged us back to indicate you've taken your heart medication this afternoon. We don't want you to have to return to the heart center, so please make sure to take your medication and let us know you have."

Does this sound like hand-holding? Does it seem like too much to ask? Based on the personal services provided in home security and other industries, the day hospitals provide personalized updates, reminders, and custom monitoring might not be far off. Indeed, to remain competitive, providing such customized attention might become vital to reducing hospital readmission rates.

At the Women's Center in a Tampa Bay hospital in Florida, when a patient arrives, she is given a cell phone. The phone only functions inside the hospital. She can take the phone to the cafeteria, gift shop, or anywhere else in the complex, knowing she will receive a call a few minutes before her appointment.

Not a huge innovation—or is it? Restaurants have employed this technique for years. In hospitals, such use of technology greatly reduces anxiety. After all, does anyone enjoy sitting around in a waiting room where the minutes hang like hours? Especially when a patient is deeply concerned about a health issue, the ability to walk around instead of sitting in a waiting room with other equally anxious patients can make a visit significantly more pleasant. Among most patients, the perception of quality at the Women's Center rises when they use the special cell phone, independent of the medical services rendered.

THE PERSON-TO-PERSON DIFFERENCE

If you give your patients the option of completing preregistration forms in advance and submitting them by mail, fax, or Internet, make sure the information actually enters your system. To prevent patients' frustration and anxiety and enhance your perceived quality, don't make them fill out forms twice.

Discuss the larger questions of personalization at your hospital. Does your hospital want patients to communicate directly with their doctors? By phone? By e-mail? Does it make sense to set aside hours for addressing e-mail? Are the same considerations being contemplated for nurses and technical specialists? This level of accessibility is new and intimidating. But configuring your IT system so your staff can communicate with patients one-on-one could prove to be mandatory in this ultracompetitive industry.

Implications for Your Hospital

What are you doing to harness IT in ways that serve consumers and help raise their perception of the quality of your services?

- Do you have an appointment reminder system in place?
- Have you captured the requisite data to electronically connect with your customers? For example, do you have their cell phone numbers and e-mail addresses?
- Do you have their permission to initiate such contact?

- Have you harnessed IT to make the patient's experience more pleasant from the time he makes an appointment?
- Can the patient preregister online? People are more comfortable doing this simple task at home than registering in a hospital or waiting room.

Once they're inside the hospital doors, what do you do to ensure patients' comfort and ease?

- Do you provide in-house cell phones so individuals are free to walk instead of being cooped up in a waiting area?
- Have you scanned a photo of the patient so your reception staff might recognize and personally greet him?
- Are your IT systems configured so the greeter knows the date of the patient's last visit? Such knowledge influences how the patient should be greeted.

Is your hospital using technology and social media in the way patients want?

- Is your hospital developing its own apps?
- Are you offering easily accessible frequently answered questions (FAQs)?
- Are you using YouTube to provide basic instructions such as how to check in or how to administer self-care following a visit?

THE INTERNET AS FIRST HEALTH INFORMATION PROVIDER

According to a study by the Pew Internet and American Life Project, a research firm that tracks the social impact of the Internet, eight in ten Internet users have searched online for health information. As of the end of 2009, the Internet ranked third after health professionals and family members as a viable source of medical information and health advice. Sixty percent of respondents said health information they found online was helpful (Fox and Jones 2009).

Doctor Tom Ferguson coined the term *e-patient* and called such patients "equipped, enabled, empowered, and engaged" (Ferguson 2007). E-patients use the Internet to research their own health conditions and those of their loved ones. The two effects of e-patients' online health research are "better health information and services, and different (but not always better) relationships with their doctors" (Fox and Fallows 2003).

What E-Patients Want to Know

When patients go online, what are they looking for? They research diseases, treatments, and, increasingly, alternative treatments. They look up information about hospitals, doctors, and insurers. Some even monitor clinical trials, gain access to medical journal articles and studies, and read details about testing procedures and outcomes.

They look for articles and features on specific diseases and problems, specific medical treatments and procedures, diet and nutrition, vitamins and nutritional supplements, exercise and fitness regimens, prescriptions and over-the-counter drugs, health insurance, alternative health treatments, specific doctors and hospitals, depression, anxiety, stress, and other mental health issues.

Consumers also seek information about environmental health hazards, drug and alcohol dependency, experimental treatments and medicines, immunizations and vaccinations, Medicaid and Medicare, and how to quit smoking.

While people aged 18 to 29 are most likely to seek information online, followed by those aged 30 to 49, the 50 and older segment is not shy about using online health information (Taylor 2002).

Surveyed e-patients reported that they would like additional information or capabilities online, including doctor-to-patient e-mail, appointment scheduling, drug interactions, decision support for tests and treatments, online diagnostic tools or "symptom finders," and better ways to connect with local resources (Fox and Fallows 2003).

Incorporating E-Medicine

Another groundbreaking use of IT in healthcare is the e-visit—a virtual, electronic doctor visit.

E-visits and other forms of telemedicine are discussed at length in Chapter 6.

The e-patient phenomenon will only intensify in the coming years. Progressive hospitals and schools, in turn, are taking action to accommodate the change, teaching medical students about working with e-patients, and building e-visits into their offerings.

When E-Patients Predominate

E-patients and e-visits can help cut costs. Research indicates patients who correspond with their doctors via e-mail effectively reduce the overall number of office visits needed. Health insurers understand this and have installed reimbursement systems for doctors who are willing to visit with patients online.

As more and more Internet-savvy e-patients take charge of their own healthcare and find providers who are willing to work with them, the field moves toward an era in which doctors can make rounds with just a stethoscope and a smartphone.

The *Journal of Participatory Medicine* (www.jopm.org) offers online peer-reviewed articles on shared healthcare decision-making. The journal examines issues related to joint decision-making between doctors and patients and how heavy patient engagement affects the outcome of a patient's healthcare. Unlike traditional medical journals, the *Journal of Participatory Medicine* carries articles from healthcare providers, insurers, employers, patients, and other players in the healthcare field.

Implications for Your Hospital

Evaluate your website and other technology.

- Have your systems been designed to help consumers assess their risk factors?
- Does your system help motivate users to make lifestyle improvements?
- Can patients easily access their own health records or family health records and gain access to personalized treatment recommendations derived from assessing their health? (See Chapter 3 for more on health records.)
- Do you provide interactive online learning tools to help optimize patient care, including information on a variety of medical conditions, treatments, recovery, and prevention and wellness?

Keeping Pace Is Impossible

No one can keep up with all medical advancements. It is simply not feasible for doctors and medical professionals today to read every available piece of health literature on every existing health condition. Patients who spend hours researching their health conditions can easily arrive at a hospital or the office of a doctor or the top specialist for their condition with more information than the provider knows. For doctors today, the shock of e-patients has worn off. They know many patients have become self-taught subject matter experts and that some of these patients have an unassailable depth and breadth of knowledge.

Are E-Patients Really at Risk?

The unregulated nature of the Internet means that e-patients risk finding outdated and incorrect health information. Medical professionals worry about the health outcomes of following inexpert online advice. However, damage caused by bad e-advice appears to be far less frequent than damage or death from real-world medical errors (Ferguson 2007). Passive patients who don't take charge of their health may be the real people at risk.

Consumers Want Connection

Providers face a new challenge from the fact that patients who use the Internet, e-mail, and smartphones are often at the head of the technology curve, far ahead of hospitals and physicians. In a 2008 study in the *New England Journal of Medicine* (DesRoches et al. 2008) fewer than one in five doctors reported using computerized medical records, and in our experience as consultants, we have observed that even fewer doctors use e-mail to correspond with patients.

Consumers are losing patience waiting for access to their own medical records and the ability to communicate online with hospitals and individual doctors. Using IT to harness e-patients' knowledge can help reduce costs, relieve burdens, and raise hospitals' perceived quality level. The prerequisite, of course, is the ability to interact in a manner that is fitting, proper, and convenient for the patient.

Through Patients Like Me (www.patientslikeme.com), which had 50,000 members as of the end of 2009, consumers can exchange personal health information and observations with others who have the same conditions they do. The founder of Patients Like Me, Jamie Heywood, says, "The amazing shift is that we've pushed out this concept of sharing . . . which is to say: if you share information about your own experience with this disease, then we can facilitate the conversation you want to have with the person in the world who is just like you" (Shapiro 2009). Finding someone who is experiencing the same treatments, side effects, and health problems as you is almost transformative.

If your doctors don't understand the power of information-sharing, how do you expect to serve e-patients effectively and make them believe your quality of care is high?

Implications for Your Hospital

Have you empowered your staff so they have resources, time, and opportunity to respond to the growing numbers and growing needs of e-patients?

- Do you provide training to doctors and hospital staff to accommodate the e-patient phenomenon?
- Does your IT enable your staff to conveniently interact online, file and use correspondence with patients, and deliver higher-quality service?
- Are such correspondence and records transferable if other professional staff is assigned to the patient's case?
- Have you explored issues of security and privacy in online correspondence between medical staff and patients?
- Are your e-visit policies clearly established, transparent, and suited to the needs of the growing ranks of e-patients?
- Do your billing systems reflect e-visits?
- Are traditional patients given the opportunity to partake in e-patient services?

TECHNOLOGY TO COLLECT EVIDENCE

Do you use IT to capture feedback about your services? When a major motion picture is due for release, critics attend special screenings and offer their reviews days before the movie is in theaters. The advertisements for the forthcoming movie are adorned with praise from the critics. For the movie's entire run, its advertising continues to include any noteworthy blurbs.

Are you collecting critical, presolicited reviews of your facility? To favorably influence future consumers, are you collecting patient testimonials and letters and online and offline evidence of your quality of care, other than the typical reports that transparency dictates you assemble?

Even if you're not currently collecting such evidence, your competitors are. It's not enough to do an outstanding job—you need to be ahead of the social media curve. Public review sites such as Yelp (www.yelp.com) and Citysearch (www.citysearch.com) encourage testimonials and provide a forum for patients to discuss their experience with healthcare providers, in the same manner as if they were rating a movie or cruise ship. The feedback given on these sites can be undependable and unreliable, but your organization can benefit by counteracting even one bad review with dozens of excellent reviews.

What are you doing to encourage your patients to offer their honest feedback in ways that can help influence others to come to your facility? Recall the last time you were in a dentist's office and you saw a wall of smiles—all those pictures of people proudly showing their teeth. What a clear indicator to the next patient who walks through the door that he's in a good place to get excellent dental care.

HOT TIPS AND INSIGHTS

- Your IT systems need to help patients maintain their medical records, assess their risk factors, and get motivated to make lifestyle improvements.
- IT and personal portable technology are redefining the hospital–patient relationship and determining which hospitals flourish.
- The coming wave of interns is savvy with smartphone technology and likely will expect your hospital to be as well.
- Doctors armed with patient EMRs have an immediate and vast potential to offer better service, improve the patient's perception of service quality, and cement long-term relationships.
- The variety of patient-facing smartphone apps your hospital can develop is unlimited and holds vast potential to solidify your market position.

CHAPTER 3

Personal Health Records

IN THIS CHAPTER:

- Personalized health records will revolutionize healthcare
- Vendor support
- Identification and security issues
- Capitalizing on opportunities

To stay competitive and relevant to all generations, healthcare providers must invest in IT that is simple, useful, informative, relevant, and accessible to the end user. This new technology must coalesce with other cost-saving initiatives to control healthcare costs. Consumers today, especially younger patients, desire access to their personal health records, demand information related to cost and quality, and nearly always make healthcare purchasing decisions based on this information.

Personal health records (PHRs) go by many names:

- Electronic personal health profiles
- Electronic personal health records
- Electronic personal health reports
- Internet-based medical records
- Online personal health records
- Personal health profiles
- Personal health reports

A PHR is controlled by the individual, who also decides who can view and use the information. By contrast, an electronic health record (EHR) or electronic medical record (EMR) is controlled by the hospital or doctor, not the patient.

Unfortunately, most Americans' PHRs are scattered among many doctors, hospitals, and insurance companies. Not many people have complete, comprehensive sets of their health records. To obtain health records, patients have to physically go to the medical office to obtain paper copies or have the records faxed.

When a patient lacks updated medical records, he is disconnected from his medical conditions and his ability to perform health maintenance is impaired. Health problems from otherwise manageable conditions escalate from lack of information. Furthermore, the lack of comprehensive PHRs leads to the duplication of paperwork for each new physician the patient sees, with a high possibility of losing or forgetting crucial information on each form. Ultimately, this could—and often does—keep patients from getting proper treatment or timely diagnoses.

NATIONAL FAMILY HISTORY DAY

In 2004, the surgeon general declared that each Thanksgiving would be National Family History Day, alternately referred to as Family Health History Day. Because many extended families are together on Thanksgiving, the holiday affords a great opportunity to talk about and write down health problems that run in the family.

A patient's family history can help doctors, physician assistants, nurses, and other health professionals provide higher-quality care because they have specific information, test results, treatment histories, and medication histories that enable them to do their jobs better. The surgeon general provides a tool for entering and sharing history, My Family Health Portrait (https://familyhistory.hhs.gov).

Entering information on My Family Health Portrait takes about 20 minutes. If the tool is filled in on Thanksgiving or another time when family members are gathered, they can help each other fill in missing information. After users enter basic family information, the portal provides a medical family tree, which can be helpful for users to share with healthcare providers.

"Discussing family health information with each other can often uncover things you never knew, simply because no one ever asked," says Surgeon General Regina Benjamin in a 2009 press release (OPHS 2009). Through open family dialogue about health history, people can learn about hereditary health conditions such as diabetes, heart disease, cancer, Alzheimer's, and mental illness in their own families.

As with other personal healthcare sites, visitors can elect to share the information with their doctors. Users must first save the information to their computers because the site does not retain the information once users log off.

National Family History Day is a campaign unknown to most Americans. It may take years for Thanksgiving to be widely linked with this campaign.

Still, the issue that the Department of Health and Human Services and the Office of the Surgeon General are supporting is clear. The highest levels of government endorse PHRs, a stance that is unlikely to change.

THE IMPACT OF ELECTRONIC PHRS

When the adoption and use of personal healthcare records catches on, it will revolutionize medicine. This revolution is on its way— the potential impact of electronic platforms on the healthcare field is astonishing.

HIPAA, Actualized

The federal Health Insurance Portability and Accountability Act of 1996 (HIPAA) guarantees consumers the right of full access to their medical records. Without the widespread popularity of publicly available platforms such as Google Health and Microsoft Health-Vault or the broad adoption of doctor-to-patient platforms such as Patient Fusion, no significant movement in which consumers took control of their PHRs could have occurred.

A Central Repository

The idea of a central repository for all of one's personal health information has been a dream at least since desktop computers became popular in the early 1980s and has gained momentum in the Internet age. Gathering information—including family histories, blood test results, cholesterol readings, and lab reports—from disparate sources and sharing it with providers lead to better health for everyone.

Some PHR sites such as myMediConnect and Revolution Health help the medical provider—no matter how technologically challenged—scan and digitize hard copies and faxes. Such documents can then become part of the PHR, enabling patients to build complete records.

For an annual fee or with per-item pricing, MyMediConnect gathers a patient's information, such as colonoscopy results, CAT scans, and X-rays, and makes it accessible in his electronic PHR. Google Health, Microsoft HealthVault, and others allow users to gain secure connections to some hospitals, pharmacies, and health insurers so users can automatically request and upload their personal records.

Most people's medical records are scattered, with data in multiple doctors' offices and prescription information at various drugstores in different geographic locations. Paper lab reports, forms, and medical receipts might be in filing cabinets, shoe boxes, or in many other inconvenient, noncentralized locations. Electronic PHRs signal the end of disorganized records.

INFORMATION ANYWHERE, ANYTIME

As online systems become more sophisticated and more people carry portable technology, the possibilities for improved healthcare accelerate. Periodic alerts to take medication, programs to track weight loss, medical appointment reminders, updates on health—all this and more is available to consumers, exactly when they want it.

If a consumer develops a bronchial infection while traveling, she can tap into her health record and identify her medications so the new doctor can check for possible drug interactions before writing a prescription. Whether a user is on vacation or at home, if a recurring medical issue flares up, he can instantly alert his doctor, request a prescription refill, identify the closest pharmacy, and be on his way with minimal effort.

Extra Help for Caregivers and Chronic Patients

Chronic health issues such as heart disease, cancer, and diabetes mandate daily management and require copious record keeping. Patients with chronic conditions may find their electronic PHRs become a tool they visit more often than Facebook—easily as satisfying, and potentially life saving. For example, diabetes patients can receive blood glucose readings at the speed of an instant message, and caregivers for sick children or elderly parents benefit from direct and instant access to medication and vaccination records.

Providers Who Are Up to Speed

As interactive capabilities become the norm, consumers seek providers who can accommodate them and abandon those who cannot. In a 2009 article in *U.S.News and World Report,* Steven Waldren, director of the American Academy of Family Physicians' Center for Health Information Technology, suggests if a patient's provider is not part of her electronic PHR team, the patient should engage in a dialogue with that provider, firmly emphasizing her desire for the provider to adopt the technology (Hobson 2009). It bears repeating: younger patients expect their healthcare providers to be electronically connected. Being the patient of a provider who is not electronically connected soon will be a nonissue. It won't happen.

A REVIEW OF PHR SITES

Electronic PHR systems are either provider-linked—available through the patient's employer, doctor, or insurer—or stand-alone. The advantage of stand-alone PHR sites is that anyone—independent of her employer, doctor, or insurer—can register and maintain her electronic PHR. If her doctor or insurer happens to use the platform, the sites enable providers to transfer information to the patient's PHR and achieve a more complete, up-to-date, and useful account.

An Early Leader in Provider Platforms

The Practice Fusion electronic health record community, which has been available to physicians since 2005, now has a patient component—Patient Fusion. Through Patient Fusion (www.patient fusion.com) users can log in, peruse and update their medical records, and connect directly with their doctors. Users can also schedule appointments, request prescription refills, share their data with healthcare providers, and e-mail their doctors directly. Note that the patient's doctor must first grant access to the medical records by signing up on Practice Fusion.

Patient Fusion is an extension of the practitioner's electronic health record in a form accessible and convenient to patients. Patient Fusion lets the user connect instantly with his PHR directly from the doctor's office, unlike Microsoft HealthVault, Google Health, and health portals offered by Aetna, Yahoo!, and AOL. At present, a patient cannot easily access his medical history at a medical office, even if the information is in electronic form. Finding, copying, and transmitting paper records to a patient is a burdensome task. With Patient Fusion, patients can monitor, update, and share their data as easily as they share other types of data through e-mail and the Web, essentially taking ownership of their PHRs. Both physicians and patients can benefit from the application.

Hospitals, medical practices, and physicians who want to use Patient Fusion can register online at www.practicefusion.com, and in about five minutes, at no cost, gain use of the site. Currently, Practice Fusion has more than 21,000 users in all 50 states, representing a potential patient population of more than 1 million. It's hard to predict which Web application will become the standard, but Patient Fusion is an early contender.

Other Leading Providers

In mid-2009, Kaiser Permanente reported that more than a third of its 8.6 million members were engaging its My Health Manager system to access their personal records, examine lab results, request prescriptions, and make appointments (Hobson 2009). Cleveland Clinic offers MyChart, a version of PHRs through which patients can manage personal data and make appointments. Dossia (www.dossia.org) helps employers provide health platforms for their employees.

MAJOR PLAYERS IN THE PHR RACE

My Health Info and HealthVault

Launched in October 2009, Microsoft's My Health Info (http:// health.msn.com/my-health-info-center) promises to supercharge electronic medical health records. It's an information management system that works in tandem with HealthVault (www.healthvault .com). HealthVault connects with health devices such heart rate monitors, scales, and pedometers to record data. The site also offers exercise and meal planners and other specialized applications focusing on fitness, weight, hypertension, health information organization, and emergency preparedness. On My Health Info, each user creates a personal dashboard on which he can record body mass index, weight, blood glucose level, and other health data.

My Health Info bills itself as "revolutionizing the medical information system" and backs up its claims by offering users real-time access to their records anywhere. It enables users to find relevant information more quickly, obtain their medical history with a single click, and engage in chats with medical experts.

The site includes many tools to help organize and monitor personal health data stored in the user's personal account on Health-Vault. My Health Info also allows users to research medical issues, receive advice from medical experts, read the latest health news, learn about nutrition, and monitor personal health conditions such as high blood pressure, high cholesterol, or diabetes.

The site offers quick tips on diet, exercise, and other health factors. Articles about many topics—knowing your body, taking precautions when you reach age 40, managing stress, and avoiding heart attacks, to name just a few—are available with one click. Users can find a nearby specialized clinic or health center, join condition-specific discussion forums, and get updates on drugs and medication. Elsewhere on the site are links to government health departments, direct contact information, a health services directory, a list of insurance providers, healthcare products, a medical education directory, and an online pharmacy.

Although My Health Info is targeted particularly to parents and caregivers, it is practical for anyone who has significant health issues, is taking multiple medications, or otherwise is interested in attaining timely, comprehensive, accurate information about his personal health.

Scott Moore, U.S. executive producer at MSN, says, "We are committed to delighting our customers with information, services,

How to Select a PHR

Consumers have many choices for PHR platforms—from doctors, prescription drug plans, and independent vendors such as Google Health. Medicare suggests that consumers ask the following in selecting a PHR platform (Medicare 2010):

- What kind of information can I store in the PHR, such as medical conditions (diagnoses), procedures, allergies, medications, and other personal information?
- Can the PHR import my claims or medical information from my health plan and/or doctors?
- What kinds of features does the PHR offer, such as the ability to print a list of my medications or conditions?
- Can I give permission to my doctors or family members to look at my PHR for me?
- What kinds of links does the PHR offer for health education information?
- If a doctor offers a PHR, can I refill prescriptions through the tool? Or make appointments?
- Is there a monthly or annual fee to use the PHR? Is there a cost for the features I want?
- What will happen to my information if I leave the health plan that offers it to me or if I change doctors?
- What will happen to my information if the company that provides the PHR goes out of business or becomes part of another company?
- What are the PHR's privacy and security policies?

and tools that keep them informed and simplify their lives" (MSN 2009). This is an ambitious goal, but My Health Info developers seem capable of achieving it.

Google Health

Google Health (www.google.com/health) is just as inviting as My Health Info. On its homepage, Google Health is forthcoming about its security policy, assuring readers that users are in control of their own data and that data is safely stored.

A simple tour shows visitors the seven simple steps involved in making a robust profile. The visitor is afforded the opportunity to create and save a Google Health profile using a free account and enter as much or as little data as he chooses related to medications, conditions, and symptoms. Users can add additional profiles for children, parents, or others.

It's unlikely the typical user would be able to report an entire medical history by himself, so Google Health has eased the process. The site has partnered with hospitals, clinics, labs, and pharmacies so patients have an easier time importing records, appointment history, prescription history, and follow-up notes from various healthcare providers. All links with such partners are safe and secure. Users simply sign in to the partner site with a username and password, and then affirm they wish to link accounts and transfer personal data to the Google Health account.

As more data is loaded into the account, users are better able view and track their medical history. Patients can see what prescriptions they've filled over the years, including the name of the drug, how it's taken, the dosage, and where it was filled. Having such data available helps providers gain a fuller understanding of a patient's condition.

When a patient adds additional data to her profile, Google Health checks to see if there are potential harmful interactions with her medical conditions, medications, and allergies.

Beyond sharing records with selected providers and family and friends, users can print their health profile in a wallet-size version to carry with them, give to others, or refer to in case of emergency.

The driving force behind Google Health is to make a patient's health information work for them. The site enables users to refill prescriptions quickly and easily online, seek a second opinion, or otherwise obtain personalized health information. Google Health maintains no financial relationship with any providers, suppliers, or other vendors listed on its site or in its databases. The user alone decides whether to share health information or contact or patronize a vendor.

Keas

In October 2009 former head of Google Health Adam Bosworth, along with George Kassabgi, launched Keas, an online health tool. Keas offers personalized care plans and focuses on explaining lab results in simple, patient-friendly language.

Keas works with partners such as CVS MinuteClinic, DiabetesMine, Dr. Greene Pediatrics, Healthwise, and Pfizer who submit their unique healthcare plans to the site. Each user chooses a plan that fits his specific health needs, such as weight and stress management, diabetes, high cholesterol, or high blood pressure.

What differentiates Keas from other online health services? It focuses on making health data understandable and translating that knowledge into an action plan for the patient. Keas aims to meet the need for specialized health information on the Internet. The combination of up-to-date, accurate personal data and timely, reliable generalized health information may usher in a new era of personal healthcare decision making.

WebMD Health Manager

The popular online health library WebMD offers an admirable PHR tool, WebMD Health Record (www.webmd.com/phr). Health Record is part of WebMD Health Manager (https://healthman ager.webmd.com/manager), a set of online tools including health assessments, messaging and reminders, lifestyle change programs, and health reference materials. The site also offers tools that track progress and help patients set goals. The detailed health assessment HealthQuotient is the starting block from which the personalized health recommendations are derived.

WebMD offers a detailed privacy policy in recognition of the sensitive nature of health information. An industry leader in privacy and security, WebMD is a participant in the TRUSTe privacy program and a recipient of the URAC privacy seal and the Health on the Net HONcode certification.

Privacy will be a predominant issue in the long-term growth of PHRs. If people don't feel their information is secure on a given site, some choose other ways of maintaining their data. Others simply opt out of the PHR movement.

More Platforms for Patients

NoMoreClipboard (www.nomoreclipboard.com) offers a basic PHR platform for free, a premium version for $9.95 a year, and a concierge version—ideal for people who have chronic conditions or see multiple doctors—for $59.95 a year. NoMoreClipboard also offers family versions of the premium and concierge plans. MyMediConnect (www.mymediconnect.net), formerly PassportMD, offers a free platform that, like NoMoreClipboard, is competitive with larger providers such as Google Health. MyMediConnect offers additional fee-based services such as document copying and scanning of X-rays and MRIs.

ON THE CONSUMER'S SIDE

MyPHR (www.myPHR.com) is provided by the American Health Information Management Association as a free public service that discusses the issue of PHRs at length. At myPHR, visitors can review options for initiating a PHR. Some of the choices are patient-maintained, others are maintained by a health provider or health plan, and a few are a combination. Consumers who choose to maintain their PHRs on their own face a considerable task. The older a patient is, the more health history she has, and hence the more data she has to round up—a time-consuming task.

As go-it-alone consumers delve further into the task of gathering their health information, they may see gaping holes in the data—missing dates of procedures and absent medication names, for example. The need for help in rounding up such data is apparent, but

---

Other Notable PHR Platforms

These sites offer innovative approaches to PHRs:

- Access My Records: www.accessmyrecords.com
- The Bartlett Personal Electronic Health Record: www.pehrtech.com
- ER Card: www.er-card.com
- MedKey: www.medkey.com
- My HealtheVet: www.myhealth.va.gov
- My Revolution: www.revolutionhealth.com/my-revolution
- Peoplechart: www.peoplechart.com
- Trip Mate: www.tripmate.com
- VitalKey: www.vitalkey.com

---

where should the client turn? Is offering such help an opportunity for your hospital? It's a question worth considering.

Medicare Pilot Programs and Pointers

Medicare itself has developed some PHR pilot programs, including

- MyPHRSC for people living in South Carolina who have original Medicare,
- Medicare PHR Choice for people living in Arizona and Utah who have original Medicare, and
- several Medicare Advantage and Part D drug plan PHR systems—availability varies by specific plan.

Currently, Medicare doesn't offer PHR platforms to people outside the Medicare program or to Medicare users not eligible for the mentioned pilot programs. Medicare directs such consumers to online information about PHRs—a variety of suggested links are available at www.medicare.gov/navigation/manage-your-health/personal-health-records/personal-health-records-overview.aspx.

Implications for Your Hospital

Most healthcare decisions are made by the individual, not the doctor. These decisions are about serious conditions such as heart disease and diabetes and lifestyle choices such as exercise, diet, and nutrition.

As more people are able to make wiser decisions about their healthcare, facilitated by the Web, the online business of consumer health is poised to take off. Is your hospital leading the way when it comes to electronic PHRs, or are you waiting to see what happens?

- Are you making strides in converting over to this feature?
- Have you chosen a platform provider?
- Are you taking precautions to ensure privacy, safety, accessibility, and transferability?
- If you were a patient in your own hospital, would you want to have an electronic PHR there?

THE INEVITABLE DOWNSIDE

Might a provider send misinformation to be used in a PHR—an incorrect billing code, a misdiagnosis, or a critical reporting error? Yes. As with all information-based systems, the quality and value of the information derived from PHRs is directly related to the quality and value of the information input. It takes effort to keep PHRs current and accurate; just how much effort is required depends on what records are already available. Certainly the early weeks and months of a PHR's assembly require more work than the later stages will. Vendors such as the Datamonitor Group (www .datamonitor.com) can assist with issues of currency and accuracy.

Identification and Security Issues

Protecting the privacy and security of PHRs while enabling the simple, ongoing exchange of information is a central concern for patients and providers. Security breaches, hacks into the system, breakdowns in data protection, and other violations of data and trust are all possible risks. More pressing than the fear of hackers is the way personal records get treated in the exchange among providers, insurers, and other parties. Ubiquitous Wi-Fi connections mean more consumers' records are subject to others' eyes.

Consumers are sensitive about some delicate PHR data, such as information about sexually transmitted diseases. Another important security area is electronic prescriptions, which require procedures to make electronic signatures legal and verifiable. Reliably matching patients' records requires unique identifying numbers. Also, PHR systems must give special security to the PHRs of public figures such as politicians and executives because of hacking risk.

Safety guarantees, seals of approval, trusted vendor certifications, and other such protections must be in place to ensure the sanctity of PHRs. The Health Privacy Project at the Center for Democracy and Technology is dedicated to looking at issues of personal privacy.

How data can be accessed is a vital issue—organizations must develop protocols that allow the requests for medical records to be quickly disseminated. Some PHR platforms allow users to delete records that don't belong or make notations when they disagree with a record or otherwise need to provide explanation. PHRs must be the property of both the individual and their providers; otherwise, there is little recourse for devising an effective system.

Accessibility and Continuity

Issues about patients' access to their own PHRs are likely to heighten in the coming decade. One basic feature doctors already want, and consumers will probably demand, is the ability to instantly see who has access to a PHR and who has actually viewed it. Every system and platform needs to guarantee users that their information is handled with the greatest care and consideration. No patient's data should ever be released without her consent.

These questions and others arise as the use of PHRs spreads:

- Who is allowed to print the PHR, and for what purposes?
- What happens when a patient severs ties with a provider?
- How easily can a patient have his record permanently deleted, if he desires?

- Is a patient's personalized record subject to data mining, even if individual identities are not disclosed?
- What role do cookies (small data files containing personal information) play in the storing of information on local computers?
- What happens when a patient dies? Should the patient's record be accessible to executors?

Implications for Your Hospital

Has your hospital developed PHR policies and procedures? There is much to consider and much to do:

- Within your own office or division of information technology, has your CIO or other top officer been involved in the PHR's progression?
- Has the officer formulated a plan for your hospital to take full advantage of forthcoming opportunities and deal with forthcoming challenges?
- Are staff members attending the latest conferences and symposiums on the PHR issue?
- Have they visited a wide variety of sites and vendors who are leading the way?
- Have they established their own electronic PHRs to become familiar with the process, understand the intricacies, diagnose potential shortfalls, and tune in to potential opportunities for your hospital?
- Is the issue of PHRs on the agenda on your weekly and monthly meetings?
- Do you have a task force, ideally a permanent one, assigned to the issue?

What about among your own staff? Are you helping and encouraging your staff to initiate and maintain their PHRs and include their families and loved ones as well?

- Have you implemented, or are you considering, a hospital-wide campaign to include all employees—in medicine, administration, and support—in the PHR adoption process?
- Are you using your own doctors to observe and refine your own record systems?
- What new ideas emerge as you become more fully involved with electronic PHRs?

Have you chosen to be a leader in this domain? Or is the issue of PHRs simply something you see as another entry in a long line of obligations and burdens? Taking a leadership position requires considering questions such as these:

- Can your hospital develop care guides for patients and other users?
- Are you working on interactive tools that help people make wiser decisions about their own health?
- Is anyone within your office or the hospital at large developing applications for smartphones?
- Are you working on health risk assessments?
- If you have a wellness program in the hospital, are the fundamentals of that program transferable to online users, particularly those who maintain PHRs?
- Do you have a health library in progress? Do you regularly update the library with self-care tools?
- Are you preparing daily health news feeds with tips that help patients take charge of their health? Such feeds can also win loyalty and appreciation for your facility.

Going further, have you considered installing a bank of phone-based counselors to help people with their medical records? After implementation, the personalized touch you offer to people who need real-time interaction with a voice on the phone, not just symbols on a screen, will differentiate your hospital. The more personalized attention you can offer to consumers, the greater the probability that they will keep you as their provider for a wide range of needs.

TO FLOURISH OR FLOUNDER?

A PHR can only be as good as the data entered into it. The less organized patients are early on, the less data they might have available to add to their files. Older people have accumulated more health history, but less of it can be easily rounded up. Could you locate a doctor you visited many years ago? Even if the doctor were still practicing, how easily could your records be located and transferred to you?

Even for a highly organized consumer who dutifully collects and files medical records, assembling a comprehensive PHR is no easy task. Most of the population is not highly organized.

The younger and more technically savvy a patient is, the more likely she'll embrace the use of PHRs. Indeed, this might be the only way young people conceive of maintaining such records.

Depending on her level of health, frequency of doctor visits, or regularity of prescription refill, a patient might engage with her PHR daily or weekly. Once a user has completed her PHR as extensively as possible, maintaining it will be relatively easy.

CAPITALIZING ON PERSONAL HEALTH RECORDS

If consumers are going to naturally gravitate to PHRs, what role should the hospital play? Should it be a provider? Should it simply be one of many players? Hospitals could approach the PHR as a tool to help solidify customer loyalty. Suppose a patient comes in for a health concern. During the stay, hospital personnel could use the PHR to troubleshoot—perhaps they see the patient's blood pressure has been rising steadily or blood glucose levels have been fluctuating outside desired norms.

Maybe the hospital upgrades its care by suggesting the patient return in the near future to take a look at an emerging issue. Or the hospital simply could call after a few months of watching PHR data to update the patient about an issue.

A Not-So-Distant Corollary

The previous example of a preventive approach to patient health is analogous to that which occurs in dental offices. The dentist takes an X-ray of the patient's teeth, then shows the patient a printout or a schematic on a screen. The dentist provides analysis: "We've noticed there's some recession around number 18, and decalcification at 14, and loose amalgam at number 11. Let's keep an eye on these and see what happens when you come back in June."

It may be unpleasant to hear about potential medical problems, but patients likely appreciate providers who pay attention. This quality care breeds patient loyalty.

The caring dentist in the example receives a regular and predictable stream of income. Even with tremendous local competition, his practice thrives. Even if a dentist across the street acquires the latest technology, is featured in the Sunday paper, and has a patient outreach program that is second to none, most of the original caring dentist's patients keep scheduling appointments just as they always have—staying loyal because they appreciate the level of care.

A hospital is not a dental practice, but there are predictable elements of human interaction upon which your organization can build a loyal customer base.

Beyond Single Episodes

Consider this scenario: a patient arrives at your hospital requiring shoulder surgery. The follow-up appointment is made at the doctor's office a mile away. Rehabilitation appointments are scheduled at a rehabilitation center a few miles in the other direction. Your hospital has no idea whether the patient shows up for shoulder rehabilitation, or for that matter, if the patient is healing properly. The only indicator your hospital or surgeon has is if the patient returns to your hospital because something goes wrong.

In this situation a PHR could play a key role in the patient's overall health and in the hospital's ability to engender loyalty. PHRs show the provider an entire spectrum of care—the patient's story is available to review and understand. This example is simple but common—think of the vast number of patients with varying conditions, some that require extensive follow-up care for months, years, or a lifetime.

Opportunities Buried in the Data

A hospital case manager who intelligently mines the data in PHRs will see opportunities to provide a continuum of care most hospitals simply haven't considered. If you contact a hospital or medical office you've visited before, staff can look up your history with them. But because that particular provider does not have your whole health picture, the advice and care they can offer you is limited. With the personal health record, the prudent provider has a compilation of your data and can more readily provide you with higher-level healthcare.

Applying the results of data mining to the long-term health of your customers benefits patients and your hospital. Examining a patient's health history and determining where problems may lie in the future is one thing. Examining a patient's ancestral history takes data mining to a whole new level. The more information you have about a patient's siblings, parents, and grandparents, the greater the chance of providing that patient with excellent healthcare now and in the future.

If a patient is aware of a family history of Parkinson's disease, prostate cancer, diabetes, breast cancer, or even simply sinus problems, you are armed with valuable information. Soon, many people will pay to have their entire genome mapped. Vendors such as 23andMe (www.23andme.com) are already providing genome mapping. For several hundred dollars, a client can learn whether he is likely to develop certain illnesses. The vendor tells the client where on Earth his genes originated. The vendor offers the client a likely picture of his health to come in the next 10 to 30 years. For some services, clients have to sign a waiver: it's not pleasant to learn a devastating condition may be in your future. When multiple family members commit to the testing, an even greater level of information in health mapping can be achieved. Such mapping will redefine PHRs, incorporating historical information and potential future issues.

Data collection can also happen through nontraditional channels. Consider Nintendo's Wii Fit, an exercise-centered video game. Every time consumers play the game, personal health information could be extracted—for example, weight and activity level for the day. The system could be devised to greet players personally and ask about any specific medical conditions. Through the simple act of playing a game, much meaningful data could be extracted and added to the patient's health record.

THE FUTURE OF PHR CONTROL

Much like what has happened in credit reporting, where Equifax, Transperian, and TransUnion control the market, and as in many other industries where consolidation has occurred, ultimately the PHR market may be controlled by a few large companies. With consolidation comes standardization of data reporting, privacy, transparency, and security—uniform design standards that facilitate the integration of personal health information and accelerate the ubiquity of PHRs.

Implications for Your Hospital

It is time to determine where your hospital will be in the health information revolution: leading, lagging, or keeping pace. Seek to embrace the secure exchange of personal health information, but do not seek to monopolize any part of the system. Ask these questions about your organization:

- Are PHRs a service area you want to explore?
- If you do not provide PHRs, can you affiliate with those who do?
- Do you encourage patients without a PHR to start one?
- Do you have counselors on hand to help initiate records, or do you at least have staff who are knowledgeable about the issue and can lend support?
- Have you sought direct affiliation with Google Health, Keas, HealthVault, or My Health Info?
- Have you explored possibilities with insurers or other private vendors who develop PHR platforms?
- Have you considered co-branding with such vendors?

Above all, strive to become a major player in personalized care, providing services, troubleshooting, and preventive maintenance that engender loyalty. Ubiquitous personal health data collection will be a reality. The time to plan for it is now.

HOT TIPS AND INSIGHTS

- Soon there will be no option other than to be electronically connected with your patients.
- The widespread popularity of publicly available PHR and doctor-to-patient platforms is accelerating consumers' ability to take control.

- Because consumers are going to naturally gravitate to PHRs, it is wise to determine the hospital's role early.
- Protecting the privacy and security of PHRs while enabling the convenient, ongoing exchange of information is both a concern and an opportunity.
- Consumers face a variety of choices when it comes to selecting a PHR platform, but you can serve as a guiding force.

CHAPTER 4

Consumer-Driven Health Plans

IN THIS CHAPTER:

- Tools and information
- Penny wise, pound foolish?
- Wellness becomes the rage

THE RISE OF CONSUMER-DRIVEN health plans is fueling the dramatic shift in healthcare: the field's focus is moving from patients to consumers. In patient-centric healthcare, the customer is a passive user with limited decision support who relies heavily on the physician and the health plan. In consumer-centric healthcare, the customer is more active and engaged in the decision-making process because he is both purchaser and user of the healthcare. Decision support comes from personal advisors, the Internet, medical staff, and patient decision aids. The physician remains a trusted source who serves as a provider and a consultant.

Consumer-driven health plans are the heart of healthcare consumerism. For the first time, consumers have the ability to take control of their own healthcare by selecting providers, services, and benefits that uniquely fit their needs and desires.

A survey conducted late in 2009 by Aon Consulting and the International Society of Certified Employee Benefit Specialists shows that 44 percent of employers offer their employees a consumer-driven health plan, up from 28 percent in 2006

(Sharon 2009). Fifty-six percent of these employers link the consumer-driven health plan to an HSA that employees can contribute their own money to, retain ownership of, and transfer if they depart from that employer.

A MOVING TARGET

A critical mass of younger career professionals will have consumer-driven health plans for their entire careers. These consumers demand more choices, actively design their benefits programs, and are eager to establish HSAs and watch them build. Consumer-driven health plans are being adopted so quickly that the magnitude of the transformation is difficult to grasp.

A consumer-driven health plan coupled with a health savings account or a health reimbursement arrangement is the wave of the future. As of January 2009, more than 8 million people in the United States had such coverage, compared to roughly 6 million in 2008, 4.5 million in 2007, 3 million in 2006, and only 1 million in 2005 (AHIP 2009).

Compelled to Spend Wisely

The consumer-driven health plan concept originated in the mid 1960s. Multiple studies have determined that as individuals take responsibility for a greater portion of their medical costs, fewer medical services are actually purchased (Wharam et al. 2007; Gerfin and Schellhorn 2006). This may seem obvious, but health insurers and employers have taken decades to fully embrace this concept.

Consumers today absorb a rising share of healthcare costs, whether or not they have consumer-driven health plans. In general, employees are paying more than ever for their own healthcare, about a third of overall costs, while the rest is usually covered by employers or insurers (Halverson and Glowac 2008, 33).

In the coming years, the employee burden is likely to grow to as much as 50 percent of personal healthcare costs. Employees will engage in an unprecedented level of consumerism. They will seek to spend their healthcare dollars wisely and stretch them as far as possible. They will vigorously pursue cost and benefit information (as discussed in Chapter 1), be more demanding, and be more likely to switch to providers who offer a better deal. Providers have the edge in retaining current customers. The relationship between a doctor and a patient is the key asset a provider possesses in the quest to provide long-term, life-cycle services to that patient.

Helping with Effective Choices

Healthcare consumerism as embodied by the rise of consumer-driven health plans might seem similar to other consumer movements, but there are notable differences. The typical healthcare consumer is bewildered by her healthcare options and the onslaught of information on the Web. The variety of plans from sponsors, health program vendors, providers, and intermediaries is daunting. The medical and administrative aspects of healthcare are excessively complex. Taking charge of individual and family health is a personal, financial, and emotional issue that can be trying.

As consumers seek to make effective choices and keep pace with plan updates, they will want help. Particularly, consumers who aren't sufficiently health literate will count on others to help steer them through the maze of consumer-driven health plans. Consumers who have been in the workforce for a decade or more may have little experience in shopping for healthcare. Younger professionals may prove to be more adept at healthcare shopping, as they are accustomed to mining information and making their own decisions.

Consumers are particularly vulnerable when something goes wrong. Their reflexive response in choosing providers under adverse conditions is to rely on the two ubiquitous decision drivers—quality and price transparency (as discussed in Chapter 1).

Tools for Health

Consumer-driven health plan vendors populate the insurance market, and a few major players have emerged through consolidation. Employers welcome the consumer-centric approach to providing health benefits because they see it as an essential way to contain costs.

For consumer-driven health plans to be effective, consumers need tools and information to make better informed decisions. The consumer-driven health plan approach encourages consumers to adopt a wellness approach to healthcare, which minimizes future health issues and associated costs, and to build equity in their plan as a by-product of making wise healthcare decisions and purchases.

The consumer-driven health plan needs to provide decision support tools to help employees choose providers who specialize in diet and nutrition, exercise and fitness, health risk appraisals, and pain management. Such plans include preventive care services to encourage employees to seek early detection and early treatment of any illness or condition. The employee is encouraged to seek providers who offer discounted fees for service.

Employers who contemplate instituting consumer-driven health plans need to ensure their employees are protected. For example, the plan has to include catastrophic insurance for the runaway costs associated with critical injury and illness. The plan needs to include an employee-funded deductible in case the reimbursement amount is depleted. Usually reimbursement is initially funded by the employer. Any unused amount at year's end can roll over tax-free to help offset future out-of-pocket costs.

HEALTH REIMBURSEMENT ARRANGEMENTS

Health reimbursement arrangements (HRAs), also known as health reimbursement accounts, are a common part of consumer-driven health plans and are usually coupled with a high-deductible health plan. Such plans currently have a minimum annual deductible of $1,150 for single coverage and $2,300 for family coverage (Rand Compare 2009). HRAs are employer-established, employer-funded benefit plans that include free preventive care for members, up to a maximum dollar amount, not charged against the deductible.

Consumers can roll over any unused funds at the year's end for future use, COBRA benefits, long-term care, or Medicare premiums. Because consumers have to pay a high deductible, they will shop around for value at a reasonable price and, hopefully, make better-informed choices about care.

HEALTH SAVINGS ACCOUNTS

Health savings accounts (HSAs) have seen a dramatic rise. According to 2009 data from the U.S. Department of Treasury, 438,000 individuals were covered by HSA-type insurance plans in 2004, whereas the department projects a minimum of 14 million HSA policies by the end of 2010.

HSAs, like HRAs, are usually coupled with high-deductible health plans. HSAs are designed to help consumers pay and save for current or future qualified medical and retiree health expenses on a tax-free basis. HSAs are owned and controlled by the consumer and, like savings accounts, accrue a small amount of interest. An HSA can be funded by the employer, the employee, or a third party, and generally costs less than traditional healthcare coverage.

Increasingly, employers are contributing to their employees' HSAs. In Aon Consulting's 2009 study, of the 56 percent of employers who contribute to employees' HSAs, nearly half contribute $500 annually, with a small percentage actually matching employee contributions.

The employee decides how to invest the money to make the account grow. Without a health insurer dictating which providers can be seen or services can be received, the consumer is in complete control and can choose any provider. Ultimately, because she is paying, the consumer presumably chooses a provider who offers high quality at a competitive rate.

HSAs are by no means a cure-all. They have no appreciable impact on the value of healthcare delivery. However, when the majority of policyholders use their funds wisely, the results are positive. Aetna's HSA subscribers tend to spend more on preventive care and experience notably lower rates of otherwise increasing healthcare costs. These subscribers also seek more information about healthcare choices, are more likely to use generic medications, and are less likely than other consumers to visit the emergency room (Porter and Teisberg 2006).

A Breed Apart?

Are consumers who establish HSAs a self-selecting bunch who are already healthy? Aetna and other insurers have seen differences in behavior among those with HSAs versus those without (Porter and Teisberg 2006). Perhaps having an HSA gives the consumer an enhanced sense of responsibility for making healthcare choices.

HSAs work best when there is competition among providers, an abundance of transparent information, and decision-making assistance. In the absence of sufficient information or choice of providers, an HSA is merely a device for shifting costs from employers to patients and restricting patients' decisions about seeking care. Evidence suggests HSAs may prompt undesirable self-rationing, where patients forego needed care to save money (Porter and Teisberg 2006).

The Long-Term Impact of HRAs and HSAs

In consumer-driven health plans, HRAs and HSAs drive consumer involvement, transparency in quality and price, and free market forces to reduce the costs of healthcare. Ultimately, consumer-driven health plans will drive health insurers to lower premiums, customize plans, and cater to consumers to retain them as customers. Consumer-driven health plans are an excellent alternative to traditional health insurance plans. However, consumer involvement depends on factors such as consumers' purchase criteria and availability of key information.

As consumers gain familiarity with HRAs and HSAs and these accounts grow significantly, issues of ownership, transferability of funds, and security will heighten. Consumers want easy access to their accounts, regardless of their employer or employment status. They might seek HSA credit for unused sick leave and vacation time, and the ability to use credit cards and debit cards when drawing from their account funds.

Implications for Your Hospital

Are you contemplating what services you can provide to the legions of consumers who will soon have consumer-driven health plans?

- Based on the demographics of your target population, do you have in place the kinds of programs customers are most likely to seek?
- How can you accentuate, price, and effectively promote your services?
- What is the potential for you to add new services to your current mix?
- Can you affiliate with organizations who offer what you do not?
- What other solutions can you devise?

DEDUCTIBLE AMOUNT MATTERS

Employees are recognizing that their employers are having a difficult time meeting rising healthcare costs. Astute employees also recognize that if they don't need to spend on healthcare now, funds can be diverted to their future needs.

While deductibles in traditional health plans often exceed $1,000, the deductible in a consumer-driven health plan can range anywhere from $1,500 to $5,500 (AHIP 2009). Thus, the consumer has an immediate incentive to shop for healthcare services that offer needed benefits without costing too much. The higher the deductible, the more likely the consumer-driven health plan will be supplemented with an HSA or an HRA, which enable employers and employees to contribute funds to meet the cost of healthcare not covered by insurance.

Booz Allen Hamilton (2007) forecasts rapid growth in the enrollment of high-deductible health plans, predicting that by 2020, approximately 60 percent of those insured through their employers will be in some form of a high deductible and high cost-sharing plan, and 20 to 25 percent of the privately insured market will be enrolled in consumer-driven health plans with an HRA or HSA.

Short-Term Savings, Long-Term Drain?

Critics suggest that high-deductible consumer-driven health plans end up costing the consumer more in the long run, because some healthcare is put off (Halverson and Glowac 2008). Consider Tom, who initiates an HSA and has a high deductible consumer-driven health plan. Tom has not previously been concerned about medical expenses, but this year he has to be. He hurt his shoulder and needs surgery and follow-up care. Suddenly costs and providers matter to Tom: How much will the surgery and follow-up care cost? Where will he go for surgery and post-operative treatment?

Later in the year, Tom starts having back pain, but it is not as pressing as the shoulder injury. In light of his high deductible, he decides not to spend any more money for a while if he can manage. He adopts a de facto program of deferred maintenance. He will put off buying medications, undergoing a physical, and having other exams for as long as he can.

Normally Tom might see a specialist for the back pain, but if the visit costs him $180 instead of the $25 copayment of his previous insurance plan, he will avoid the expense. Deferred maintenance and reluctance to take action eventually put him in trouble when the pain gets worse. The cost of attaining proper treatment now is far more than the cost of paying a little bit along the way.

Implications for Your Hospital

If the trends continue, an explosion in the number of consumer-driven health plans is coming. Many consumers will seek to lower their premiums and build their HSAs.

- As consumers' HSA balances rise, how will your service mix shift to meet the new opportunities?
- Do your top medical professionals and key executive staff understand the need to capitalize on these opportunities?
- How are providers outside of your region reacting to the growth of consumer-driven health plans?
- Could you employ, affiliate with, or form partnerships with massage therapists, naturopaths, chiropractors, and acupuncturists whose patients often spend money from HSAs?
- What are the innovators in your region offering, and what do they charge for such services?
- Have you surveyed your customer base to determine what additional services they would like?
- Who can design such a survey, administer it, and interpret the data?

PATIENT DECISION AIDS

Patient decision aids are tools specifically designed to help individuals make decisions about their healthcare options. Aids can be paper or electronic and should review the pros and cons of each available treatment method for a condition, using evidence-based information. The aids help patients quickly get information, gain clarity, and identify the personal value of certain health choices. Healthwise's self-care guides (www.healthwise.org) are good examples of patient decision aids. Decision aids help all consumers, especially those with consumer-driven health plans who make major decisions about surgery and other procedures.

Patient decision aids are not designed to point patients in one direction or to diminish the role of person-to-person consultation with care providers. They make patients better informed and more aware of the impact of their decisions. Some 500 patient decision aids are available or are in some stage of development (IPDAS 2009).

Consumers have difficulty determining whether a particular decision aid is a reliable source of health information. The International Patient Decision Aids Standards (IPDAS) Collaboration (www.ipdas.ohri.ca) seeks to establish internationally approved guidelines for determining the quality of patient decision aids.

As patient decision aids proliferate, increase in quality, and become more user friendly, consumer-driven health plan holders and other consumers will have another tool with which to make healthcare choices.

OPTING FOR WELLNESS

Recent history has shown that using wellness programs reduces consumers' health plan premiums. In Deloitte's 2008 Survey of Healthcare Consumers, 83 percent of respondents showed interest in participating in a wellness program offered by their insurance company, employer, or other health plan if it reduced their premiums or lowered their copayment burden.

The more involved a consumer is in healthcare decision making, the more likely he is to have favorable health outcomes and lower costs. Of the Deloitte survey respondents, 61 percent wanted tools that offer individualized tips for improving their health. Many also wanted the ability to monitor, assess, and manage their health and would pay extra for such tools. A surprising 53 percent would employ the services of a health or lifestyle coach if it were part of their health plan.

Consider Teri, who is in excellent condition and has been in control of her own health for years. She has an HSA with a significant balance. How does that alter the service mix you consider offering? A consumer like Teri might seek chiropractic care, massage therapy, or her own health coach. She might patronize a retail clinic. She would be enthusiastic to have a health club membership as part of her plan.

Wellness Center Opportunities

With the growing recognition that a patient's health and well-being extend beyond office visits, medical procedures, prescriptions, and basic nutrition, many hospitals consider offering health and wellness components to their staff, customers, and the community at large.

Health and fitness centers are possible revenue sources that represent a form of wellness, supplementing many of the benefits that traditional medical facilities provide. With some 15,000 health and fitness centers across the United States, hospitals have many opportunities for affiliation. There are nearly 1,000 hospitals throughout the United States and Canada already associated with fitness centers (Medical Fitness Association 2010).

EXEMPLARY CENTERS

Hospital wellness centers often encompass a variety of services and features that go beyond mere fitness centers. Services such as massage, acupuncture, counseling, rehabilitation, stress reduction programs, pastoral care, and meditation sessions can be part of the mix. Examining ideal wellness centers can yield ideas for your organization's own endeavors.

Piedmont Hospital Health and Fitness Club

The Piedmont Hospital Health and Fitness Club in Atlanta, Georgia, is notable for its range of amenities and for the personal attention it pays its members. The 25,000-square-foot facility offers strength-training equipment; cardiovascular exercise equipment; lap and therapy pools; an impressive variety of classes, including targeted classes for people with COPD, cancer, and other conditions and diseases; and deluxe locker rooms.

Working with an exercise physiologist, each new member completes a comprehensive personal fitness profile and receives a unique exercise prescription. In a mission mindful of its affiliation with the hospital, the club focuses on optimal health maintenance, fitness and nutrition, disease prevention, and injury rehabilitation. Members include those who live and work nearby and Piedmont employees, and the club is open to all ages and fitness levels.

Galter LifeCenter

Galter LifeCenter (http://galterlifecenter.org) bills itself as Chicago's premier medical fitness center. The center is a member of the Medical Fitness Association and is affiliated with Swedish Covenant Hospital. The facility offers educational events about healthy living, dozens of fitness classes, and a range of integrative therapy such as massage and acupuncture. The center also offers health screenings including lipid profiles, blood pressure readings, metabolic panels, and more. The two pools house aquatic classes for adults, children, and families. Among other added values for members, the center runs member appreciation events and offers a newsletter and online wellness community.

The Center for Healthy Living

The Center for Healthy Living at Oklahoma University Medical Center in Oklahoma City conveniently centralizes many health services. The center comprises medical offices, an ambulatory surgery center, the Oklahoma Center for Athletes, and a 65,000-square-foot fitness facility called the Health Club. The club is remarkable because of its medical focus. It is staffed by medical professionals and includes a unique feature—fitness and nursing supervision stations.

Methodist H.E.A.L.T.H. Club

Methodist Hospital, based in Henderson, Kentucky, hosts the Hospital Employees Accomplishing Long Term Health (H.E.A.L.T.H.) Club. The club is a great example of starting a wellness movement within the hospital itself. The club is free to hospital employees, physicians, retirees, volunteers, hospital board members, and members' spouses.

Implications for Your Hospital

Today's adults fully understand that exercise, lifestyle choices, and an integrated approach to health and wellness are the best remedies against illness, disease, and infirmity. Here are some issues to explore if you're considering adding a health club, health and fitness center, or wellness center:

- How many of your customers would patronize the center?
- What is the potential revenue? Factor in various levels of membership fees and a la carte services.
- Can you integrate the center with other hospital-based programs to increase patronage, loyalty, and revenue?
- Which facilities in your area might be suitable partners?
- Which facilities within your existing structures might be suitable for conversion?
- How will such a center contribute to your overall brand, mission, community outreach, and ability to compete locally and regionally?
- Can you afford to ignore this opportunity?
- What existing models can you learn from?
- Who should lead this initiative?

A BOLD INITIATIVE

What if you initiated a consumer-driven health plan for your own employees? Consider Alegent Health, whose commendable transparency was discussed in Chapter 1. Alegent, a nonprofit healthcare system, launched such a plan for its own employees. In 2005, Alegent's executives were discussing how to treat its workforce as consumers, and an idea emerged. Alegent would shift payment responsibilities from insurers to consumers—its own employees—through a consumer-driven health plan. Such a move would give employees a strong sense of control over their healthcare choices. With this move, Alegent became a pioneer among providers (Halverson and Glowac 2008).

Implications for Your Hospital

Developing your own consumer-driven health plan is a bold strategy. In addition to generating cost savings for your hospital staff, it helps you understand your customers' motivations and makes you better able to serve them.

- Have you examined other providers' consumer-driven health plans?
- What has been your experience thus far in treating patients who have consumer-driven health plans? Can your patient records or other data show you which patients have such plans?
- What mix of services and benefits do health plan customers opt for?
- How feasible is offering a consumer-driven health plan to your staff?
- How many people would be involved in the plan?
- From what benefits may employees choose?

HOT TIPS AND INSIGHTS

- Consumer-driven health plans are at the heart of healthcare consumerism, and soon your typical patient will have one.
- Establish the service mix you can provide to consumers who have consumer-driven health plans.
- Determine how to capitalize on the opportunities that come from consumers with high HSA balances.
- Help consumers navigate healthcare options and information by becoming the clear provider of choice.
- To what degree can you support consumers' quests for wellness? Wellness is what all consumers ultimately want.

CHAPTER 5

Concierge and Retail Medicine

IN THIS CHAPTER:

- The quest for convenience and accessibility
- Don't get angry, get strategic
- Your current retail businesses

EMERGENCY ROOM WAIT TIMES have drastically increased (Horwitz and Bradley 2009). The crowding in ERs is not because of the large numbers of uninsured people, although they do make an impact. Many patients come to the ER because they have no access to their primary care doctor. While it's unpleasant to wait around in the emergency room for three to five hours, the payoff is that you're treated the same day. For patients, accessibility is nearly everything.

Such accessibility issues make it easy to understand the appeal of concierge and retail medicine. These forms of convenience-based delivery provide primary care, preventive health, wellness and fitness services, self-care, and self-diagnostics. Convenient care's values are ease of use and accessibility in place and time.

Let's explore consumer-driven movements and how your hospital can benefit from the opportunities they pose.

CONCIERGE MEDICINE

Concierge medicine involves a direct financial relationship between doctors and patients. Doctors reduce their caseloads and offer patients unrushed, specialized care and easier access than in traditional practices. Concierge medicine goes by many names:

- Boutique medicine
- Direct care
- Executive health programs
- Gold card medicine
- Gold key medicine
- Platinum practices

Attractive to Consumers

Despite the sluggish economy of the last several years, many people are willing to pay out-of-pocket for healthcare. A concierge practice caters to this market. The patient pays an up-front fee for easy access to the doctor and his staff. An annual fee, ranging from $200 to $2,000 or more, is usually required.

Concierge patients can make appointments without going through extensive phone trees. Lead times for appointments are not long. The office staff speak to patients as if they know them, and usually they do. Patients have all their medical questions answered, receive specialized health communications, and are likely to get a more thorough annual physical than in traditional practices. Doctors may also provide discounts on needed medical products.

Consumers seek conveniently located services without the nuisances associated with a larger provider. Beyond greater access, they seek quality services and wide-ranging amenities such as an attractive, less crowded reception area; a better-decorated facility, and more personalized interaction. Concierge practices may offer

24-hour pager capabilities or the cell or home phone number of the physician.

Some concierge practitioners accompany patients to appointments with other specialists and provide out-of-office care. Some make house calls or offer Saturday appointments, extended evening hours, and priority arrangements as needed.

Attractive to Doctors

Concierge medicine works well for primary care physicians and specialists who have good, long-standing relationships with many patients. Doctors who recognize that giving patients access is as vital as any other aspect of the relationship—even quality of care—will likely contemplate the advantages of establishing concierge care practices.

Higher costs, increased administrative burdens, decreasing reimbursements from third-party payers, and a host of other factors put pressure on doctors in traditional practices. Some doctors with a healthy tolerance for risk are willing to see fewer patients at a set annual fee in exchange for the delivery of higher quality services and amenities. Most of these doctors opt to not participate in arrangements with third-party payers such as private insurers and Medicare.

Doctors who establish successful concierge medical practices gain a better quality of life. Instead of seeing more than 3,000 patients a year, they see perhaps half of that. Patients pay cash, something every doctor prefers.

A High-Tech Tool for Concierge Practices

HelloHealth, a Web-based practice-management platform (www .HelloHealth.com), helps doctors set up their own direct-pay practices. The platform includes an electronic medical record and interactive communication tools enabling physicians and patients to correspond online and face-to-face. Registered patients can connect with their doctors via e-mail, instant messaging, phone, or video chat. Patients can schedule appointments, ask questions, and receive test results with relative simplicity. They don't need as many office visits because of such excellent alternative access. Freedom from insurance regulations means easier physician access and patient-centric care.

Implications for Your Hospital

Could you give concierge practices office space and make it attractive to operate within your hospital? This partnership can result in more business for your organization. Most hospitals are in central, well-known locations, and a private doctor's office within a hospital is convenient for patients because they can access your facility's services at the same time as a doctor's visit. Doctors tied into your system will make referrals and care recommendations that your hospital can fulfill.

The real challenge is addressing the existing relationship that you have with your current medical staff. It's hard enough to keep your doctors happy, and offering concierge services might not help. Still, you need to consider the option. As concierge medicine becomes more popular, it is wise to seize the opportunity to benefit from these practices, rather than passively losing more business to them.

Could you establish a relationship with physicians who may eventually start a concierge practice? Check for any existing medical staff bylaws that prevent you from offering innovative services. Your bylaws may expressly forbid concierge activities. If so, consider these questions:

- Does this prohibition reflect the reality of the times?
- Who is part of the amendment process?
- Do those involved truly understand the ultracompetitive healthcare arena?

- Do your doctors understand the necessity of being flexible to keep the hospital viable?

Sometimes a little compromise by everyone, for the good of the whole, is not just a smart idea but essential.

If you know that area physicians are going to lure away your best cash customers with their concierge practices, explore offering your own form of concierge care. For example, 63 percent of U.S. adults are overweight or obese (Flegal et al. 2010). How can you assist this population? People with consumer-driven healthcare plans (detailed in Chapter 4) will likely choose exercise classes, health clubs, weight-loss spas, and other weight-reduction services as part of their cafeteria plan benefits. Health savings accounts owners also might choose to spend their money on fitness-related programs, gym memberships, and diet and nutrition counseling. If you can offer fitness, diet and nutrition, or counseling services on your premises, you might be able to compete with boutique services that offer the same. You could capture customers who wouldn't otherwise patronize your hospital, and you could gain revenue while exposing those people to the rest of your hospital's facilities.

THE RISE OF RETAIL MEDICINE

Consumers are eager to explore retail and alternative medical services. The business model of retail providers is built on customer convenience. Who wants to wait a week to see a doctor when you can drive to Walmart or Target, see somebody within minutes, pay with your credit card, and be done? The prospect of getting a diagnosis, treatment, and prescription; having that prescription filled; and shopping—all before leaving the store—is enticing. Such multitasking is alluring. In one survey of 1,000 people, 42 percent indicated that they visit the supermarket, cleaners, or bank in the same trip as visiting a doctor's office (Halverson and Glowac 2008).

The driving force continues to be convenience. Many walk-in clinics without on-site pharmacies still stock the 50 or so most common medications. Others offer free prescription delivery.

Receptive Consumers

Deloitte's 2008 Survey of Healthcare Consumers revealed that consumers are receptive to innovations such as retail clinics. Sixteen percent of consumers indicated that they had used a walk-in clinic in a drug store, retail store, shopping center, or other retail setting, while another 34 percent said they would be willing to do so.

The fact that customers value convenience, perhaps above all else, shows again in the Deloitte survey's responses. Eighty-three percent of respondents wanted same-day appointments and a surprising 26 percent would be willing to pay more for such access.

Among respondents aged 30 to 49, nearly half had used a walk-in clinic. It's clear that the younger the consumer, the more likely she will opt for retail medical services. Generation Y consumers in particular prefer to shop around for medical care, primarily on the Web, finding the right mix of price, quality, location, and convenience.

Public Health and Hospital Benefits

Walking in and getting an immunization at a retail clinic is more convenient than making a traditional appointment at a doctor's office. In an ideal world, hospitals and their expert medical staff could focus more attention on patients with greater health issues while Walmart, Target, and others handle minor sprains, scratches, sniffles, and other bandage-type fixes.

With their low flat fee and no insurance requirement, retail medical stores attract people who would have otherwise sought no medical attention.

The rise of retail clinics may result in more referrals for hospitals and primary care physicians when consumers learn from clinic personnel that they need to seek treatment in a traditional medical office for their condition.

Welcome to Walmart

When Walmart announced in 2007 its plans to add some 400 retail medicine clinics within its stores by 2010, hospital executives were skeptical whether patients would embrace the retailer as a healthcare provider. The gargantuan retail chain also announced the plan to put retail medicine in as many as 2,000 stores by 2014— amounting to clinics in two-thirds of its U.S. locations. Though the economy slowed the retailer's expansion plans—as of late 2010 there were fewer than 100 clinics in Walmarts—the retail clinic model is still viable and intriguing.

Walmart doesn't employ any of the healthcare professionals who staff the clinics it hosts, nor does Walmart have any control over how the healthcare services are provided within the clinics. The clinics are wholly owned and operated by independent companies who have arrangements with Walmart.

Services vary by clinic and can include treatments for acne, bladder infections, earaches, the flu, insect bites and stings, minor wounds, sinus infections, upper respiratory infections, and warts; blood sugar and cholesterol testing; common vaccinations; and physicals for camp or school.

Most clinics are open seven days a week and for extensive hours during the day, mirroring the hours of the host store. Walmart, like other entrants into the retail medicine marketplace, provides excellent information on price: price charts greet customers as they arrive. The typical cost at a Walmart medical clinic is $65 or less. Customers may call and discuss pricing in advance. The process is streamlined. No appointments are necessary, and patient data is all electronic.

Beyond the Big Box Stores

Today almost 1,200 retail clinics exist across 42 states. Major players in addition to Walmart are MinuteClinic (in CVS pharmacies), Target, Take Care (in Walgreens pharmacies), and the Little Clinic (in select Southeast, Southwest, and Ohio grocery stores).

The AeroClinic (www.theaeroclinic.com) operates clinics in airports. The company started in 2007 with clinics in Hartsfield-Jackson Atlanta International Airport and Philadelphia International Airport, and plans to expand. The clinics provide well care, prescription services, and treatment for minor maladies.

INDUSTRY REACTIONS TO THE RISE OF RETAIL

Hospital stakeholders likely want to react to retail medicine and compete directly in the marketplace, but their hands are tied because of their unique relationship with their physicians. Some physicians strongly oppose retail medicine because they believe that only physicians can provide quality care in the correct setting.

What if a registered nurse takes care of patients in a retail clinic? Doctors argue that RNs can treat simple problems, such as an ear infection or strep throat, but may not be aware of larger issues, such potential heart conditions associated with that strep throat. Doctors use such potentially hazardous scenarios to justify their belief that no allied health professionals should treat patients unsupervised.

However, safety steps are in place. Every retail clinic is affiliated with a medical doctor. Every retail patient has her record reviewed by a physician who signs off on the review; it's required by law.

As more clinics adopt the retail approach and more customers forsake typical healthcare insurance copayment or deductible procedures, traditional providers may have to offer comparable fee arrangements. Hospital executives understand the revenue threat that retail medicine represents. Soon Walmart, Walgreens, Target, and a host of others will have a strong hold on the primary care market and be patients' first encounter with a primary caregiver.

After the medical community's initial resistance weakens, the collective desire of consumers will prevail. You can't fight consumers, so you might as well join them.

THE FUTURE OF RETAIL MEDICINE

As consumer-driven health plans prompt more consumers to seek out maximum healthcare bang for their buck, they will increasingly explore retail medicine. This same trend will occur among those with health savings accounts. Retailers already have a huge lead helping customers track their expenses, manage receipts, and maintain personal health records.

Walk-in clinics likely will contemplate expanding operations to provide home monitoring tools and medical devices. While these have traditionally been offered through professional services, retail clinics could make major inroads in this market.

Such services will strengthen the appeal of retail clinics to the dollar-conscious consumer and increase the potential revenue loss for hospitals that would prefer to pretend that retail services are unworthy.

Implications for Your Hospital

In the United States, there is no such thing as a national healthcare provider. All healthcare is regional or local, although patients may opt to fly across the country or around the world for treatment.

Large retailers want to partner with a group that could instantly put healthcare in 400 or 4,000 of their stores.

If physician resistance and existing bylaws were not in the way and you could launch conveniently located retail care sites within your hospital or nearby, would you? If you could affiliate with retail stores such as Walmart and Target, would you? And should you?

Examine the three counties closest to you. Could you make arrangements to be in a number of retail stores? This would create visibility and exposure for your brand, create a pipeline of referrals, add additional revenue, and enable you to be a player in what is going to be a long-term and lucrative field.

If you don't establish your presence in retail superstores and other outlets, entities such as MinuteClinic and Take Care will. The next time you meet with the top officers of your hospital, the board, or your committee, pose the following questions:

- Can we afford to ignore retail medicine any longer?
- If we have made some explorations, is it time to step up the action?
- Can we launch a prototype in the next 6 to 12 months?
- What retail services are we best positioned to offer given the demographics of our local market?
- What strategies can we devise to reduce resistance and possibly engender support from our physicians?
- What are the key business obstacles?
- What existing resources can we use for optimal gain in this emerging healthcare delivery vehicle?
- Who within our organization has experience in retail medicine? Whom can we hire or affiliate with who has the requisite experience?
- In what other ways can we extend our brand?

HOSPITALS ARE ALREADY IN THE RETAIL BUSINESS

While healthcare facilities in retail outlets are fairly new, hospitals have been in the retail business for decades. Gift shops, pharmacies, and coffee shops earn hospitals an average of a half million dollars per year, estimates Gary Paquin, cofounder and executive vice president of healthcare retail consulting firm Paquin Healthcare Companies. That amount could be greatly expanded. Paquin suggests that the addition of health-related retail businesses—such as health-food markets, massage therapy businesses, and weight-loss clinics—could pump up a hospital's revenue by $5 million to $15 million annually (Sanders 2007).

The key to effective on-site retail sales is a keen focus on the consumer. The store's design and layout and your employees' knowledge are the critical elements influencing a consumer to pay for your hospital's retail goods and services.

Some hospitals have devised their own branded vitamin supplements; others offer a variety of retail notions to sell in their gift shops. Mindy Thompson-Banko's 2008 book *Beyond the Gift Shop: Boost Revenue, Your Brand, and Patient Satisfaction with Strategic Healthcare Retail* (Health Administration Press, 2008) is helpful in further exploring your hospital's retail future.

Providing Medical Equipment and Supplies

Another growing market for in-hospital retail is the provision of medical equipment and supplies. Historically, hospitals played little or no part in patients' needed follow-up care equipment, leaving the task to drugstores, wholesale medical suppliers, and specialty retail suppliers. Online vendors are capturing an increasing, sizable share of the medical supply market.

Just as hospitals can expand their traditional retail offerings, opening a medical equipment shop could be profitable. This type

Retail Services in Hospitals

Here are some of the services and specialty stores showing up in hospitals—as independent firms that pay rent to the hospital, or as part of the hospital's own operations:

- Acupuncture
- Aromatherapy service shops
- Art and dance studios
- Baby photography services
- Chiropractors
- Contact lens stores
- Cosmetic surgery centers
- Dental and orthodontic practices
- Gourmet food shops
- Health-book stores
- Health-food markets
- Massage services
- Optical shops
- Pharmacies
- Prosthetic suppliers
- Smoking cessation courses
- Specialty cancer shops offering wigs and scarves
- Specialty cosmetic centers
- Weight-loss classes

of shop would be considered a convenience to many patients, who otherwise would have to search for the products elsewhere, and the patients would trust that the hospital was stocking the appropriate items.

Running a medical equipment shop is no small operation—you need the right people, procedures, and investment—but it can pay off. Thompson-Banko's book is a valuable reference on this topic.

Implications for Your Hospital

Consider the annual number of patients you treat and the annual total patient visits to your hospital.

- How many patients require equipment or medical supplies for follow-up treatment?
- How much does the typical patient spend on such equipment?
- What is your patient population's total annual estimated follow-up expenditure?
- How much of that revenue total could you capture by entering this arena?

You must address long-term traditions, local restrictions, and other factors before medical equipment and supply sales can become a profit center. Still, the potential is intriguing and, in this era of hyper-competition, not one to be overlooked.

HOT TIPS AND INSIGHTS

- Patients in need of medical attention go to the emergency department because they do not have access to their primary care doctor or do not have a primary care doctor—access is key.
- Comparatively speaking, the United States is a wealthy country, and a sizable segment of the population will pay out of pocket for accessible healthcare.
- The concierge arrangement is attractive to doctors in many ways. Doctors profit from patients' annual fees. Can you emulate this?
- Retail medicine will inevitably see tremendous growth in the coming decade.
- Your hospital is already in the retail business and other lucrative opportunities abound. What can you do to affiliate with retail operations at arm's length or to or accommodate them within your own facilities?

CHAPTER 6

Telemedicine

IN THIS CHAPTER:

- What is telemedicine?
- A ready-made constituency
- Online providers and patients
- Remote monitoring

IF A PICTURE IS WORTH A thousand words, a video is worth at least ten times that many. Telemedicine uses two-way video, wireless phones, e-mail, and other telecommunication technology to connect doctors and patients. Telemedicine began more than 40 years ago in some hospitals that extended care to patients in remote areas; it is now spreading wider because of technological advances (ATA 2010). Telemedicine helps providers, specialty departments, private physicians, and home health agencies support consumers at home and at work.

Telemedicine most readily supports four basic services:

1. Primary care and specialist referral services
2. Remote patient monitoring
3. Consumer medical and health information
4. Medical education

These services can be delivered through network programs, point-to-point connections, monitoring centers, and Web-based e-health patient service sites.

Telemedicine offers many benefits:

- Improved access to healthcare for patients in remote locations
- Cost efficiencies through enhanced management of chronic diseases
- Reduced travel times
- Shorter and fewer hospital stays
- Shared health professional staffing

Telemedicine reduces patient stress by minimizing travel and benefits patients by giving them access to providers.

The American Telemedicine Association (ATA) (www.american telemed.org), based in Washington, DC, is the leading advocate group for telemedicine. Established in 1993, the association has more than 2,000 professional and corporate members. The ATA works with medical societies, industry and technology groups, and government officials to remove barriers to the advancement of tele-medicine. The association holds an annual meeting and commercial exposition to promote and advance telemedicine worldwide.

Let Us Count the Ways

For providers, the advantages of telemedicine are clear. It's often less expensive to provide care in a patient's home than in a hospital. If hospitals do more home care, they can avoid having to make additional brick-and-mortar investments and generate revenue from treating individuals who otherwise would not patronize them. The hospital space freed up by home care can be used for outpatient services, creating more revenue.

With the right technology installed in their homes, consumers can receive many services remotely, under the caring supervision of your organization's healthcare experts. Blood sugar testing and heart rate monitoring are two examples.

Demographics Support Telemedicine

As the World War II generation and the baby boomers age, the number of octogenarians and septuagenarians will rise accordingly. Senior citizens embrace telemedicine because of the array of advantages it provides. These patients can make quick stops at your affiliated retail clinic or concierge practice, gather needed supplies, and continue to be served primarily by your staff via a longer-term telemedicine arrangement.

Intel Takes the Plunge

As the mighty microchip grows more powerful and the market for home medical and monitoring equipment takes off, one out of two homes in America might soon contain sophisticated health-monitoring equipment. Recognizing this eventuality, tech leader Intel's healthcare division is promoting telemonitoring with their Intel Health Guide, which connects older or critically ill patients in their own homes to care teams at the health organization. Patients participate more actively in their own health, and the care team can remotely manage patients' care (Intel 2010).

Liked and Valued

A 2008 study in the *Journal of Telemedicine and Telecare* tracked 16 terminally ill patients with cystic fibrosis. Some patients received standard care alone, while others received standard care along with telemedicine. The latter group was provided high-speed Internet connection and videoconferencing equipment.

The telemedicine patients tuned into a weekly videoconference that addressed clinical assessment, offered psychological support, and enabled discussion opportunities with any of the professional staff. After six months, the telemedicine patients' body images significantly improved and the patients reported liking and valuing the videoconferencing program. The study concluded that use of telemedicine could help specialists better support patients and their families and had the potential to reduce patients' clinic attendance (Wilkinson et al. 2008).

Implications for Your Hospital

Have you already begun exploring the potential for telemedicine? Who is best able to head up this task force?

- What are the demographics of your region, and who is currently underserved?
- How can you expand your target market in providing telemedicine services?
- Which vendors can you affiliate with to help equip patients' homes for telemedicine?
- What are the potential revenues for adding this service?
- Is it feasible to establish a mobile nursing force?
- What is the cost-benefit ratio of equipping vans for a mobile nursing service?
- How can you use 4G wireless to offer new services?

YOUR TELEMEDICINE PRACTICE UNIT

Establishing an effective telemedicine division necessitates planning, coordination, and maintenance. In *Redefining Health Care,* Michael E. Porter and Elizabeth Olmstead Teisberg state, "Without common information, shared practice structures, common training, common management oversight, and personal relationships among the members of the team, the ingredients to make distance medicine truly effective are missing" (2006, 199). However complex, the venture is worth exploring.

Envision a new department of your hospital focused solely on providing telemedicine services, staffed with physicians who devote 100 percent of their time to remote patients in touch via video, webcam, e-mail, and phone. These doctors are supported by nurses trained as telemedicine facilitators.

Telemedicine enables physicians to have a more predictable schedule, particularly physicians who work in intensive care units. Sentara Health in southeastern Virginia deployed telemedicine technologies within their ICUs, monitoring their ICU beds remotely from one central location. Nurses may also benefit. A well-developed system deflects late-night calls away from on-call doctors onto the dedicated staff empowered to provide remote services.

Beyond providing a highly practical and worthwhile service to your consumer base, telemedicine can prove to be a profitable venture. Providers using telemedicine find that the cost per patient has declined. Sentara's per patient ICU cost declined by $2,150 and Sentara realized an overall ROI of 155 percent on its investments in telemedicine within the ICU (Beckley 2003).

THE ONLINE DOCTOR WILL SEE YOU NOW

Telemedicine is changing healthcare in wondrous ways. Patients can log on to online clinics without an appointment and connect with a doctor in a matter of minutes. Employers are enthusiastic about such services because they greatly decrease absenteeism, especially for relatively minor issues (Swift MD 2008). Telemedicine has been shown to reduce healthcare costs and increase efficiency (ATA 2010). Such access is often a viable substitute to a long and involved visit to an emergency room. A patient can find the appropriate doctor, chat with her online, and describe or show his medical concern.

Initial fears that providing care that wasn't face-to-face would backfire and lead to misdiagnosis, poor treatment, and lawsuits have not proved true. Remote patients are typically confident in their ability to listen to and follow the advice of remote physicians (Konschak and Flareau 2008).

A Healthy Hawaii

The Hawaii Medical Service Association has made telemedicine services available to its members and other Hawaii residents. Because Hawaii is composed of numerous islands, access to medical care poses an issue. Now patients in remote locations have around-the-clock access to basic healthcare that simply wasn't available before. Boston-based company American Well supplies the technology.

More than 150 doctors from throughout the state participate in this online healthcare program. Doctors are scheduled throughout the week to minimize patients' wait times. Even if a doctor has never worked with a patient before, the ability to pull up his medical records and communicate in real time allows the online doctor to diagnose and prescribe treatment in most situations.

Thousands of Hawaiian Medical Service Association members have registered for online services. Nonmembers may also create accounts, enter their medical history, and establish a record. Thereafter, they pay a per-visit nonmember premium.

U.S. Army mCare

To meet the healthcare needs of the many veterans returning from Afghanistan and Iraq, the U.S. Department of Veterans Affairs has begun using a telehealth program called mCare. The health of veterans with traumatic brain injuries and other serious injuries is monitored through an application on their cell phones. The veterans keep in touch with doctors and nurses using voice, text, and pictures. The application stores their personal health information. Through a Web portal, patients report their sleeping habits and moods to their health case managers, and mCare users also receive appointment reminders and health tips.

Other Telemedicine Ventures

MDLiveCare (www.mdlivecare.com) has more than 100,000 members, who pay a flat fee for an online visit with a primary care provider, therapist, or specialist. Members do not have to be covered by a health plan.

SwiftMD (www.swiftmd.com) is a phone and Internet service that prides itself on a quick response to patients—usually within 30 minutes, 24 hours a day.

HelloHealth (www.hellohealth.com), featured in the discussion of concierge practices in Chapter 5, is for patients without health insurance. Rates and payment schedules vary based on which doctor the patient chooses. Members can see their doctors' schedules and make their own appointments. Visits can be in person or through e-mail, instant messaging, or video chat.

Ask the Doctor (www.askthedoctor.com) does not provide medical care, but answers patients' medical questions online. The service prides itself on simplicity, both in language and access to technology. Questions are answered in everyday language rather than medical jargon, and connecting to a doctor is straightforward.

Doctor George Says (www.doctorgeorge.com) is a pool of medical doctors who offer health advice and recommendations through e-mail and in a chat room. The site also houses a large medical library, and its homepage features breaking health news from Reuters.

Mayo Clinic has partnered with ST Microelectronics to create a platform for remote monitoring of patients with heart disease. Through the platform, the heart patient wears a small device that monitors his breathing rate, heart rate, physical activity, and other activities. The technology reduces medical visits and costs and may detect health problems early.

PEDIATRIC TELEMEDICINE

The pediatric critical care telemedicine program at UC Davis Children's Hospital is the first in the United States to offer immediate assistance to injured and acutely ill children. Employing videoconferencing, this telemedicine program serves children throughout northern California and offers real-time remote consultation and evaluation in specialties such as cardiology, emergency medicine, child development, and child abuse. The program is particularly useful for families in rural areas whose local healthcare facilities lack access to such specialists.

Parents can stay in touch with their hospitalized children through UC Davis's Family-Link program. Employing a television set, a standard phone line, and a special camera and phone combination unit, the system allows parents and children to see and talk with each other.

At www.drgreene.com, pediatrician, professor, and author Alan Greene and his team of experts provide information and advice about children's health. In the bimonthly series "Conversations with Doctor Greene," Greene offers articles on topics such as starting solids, the flu, eco-friendly toys, labor and delivery room issues, and much more. Greene provides video replays of his guest appearances. The site also offers a live chat where registered visitors can join the online discussion with a simple click.

TELEMEDICINE FACILITATORS

A growing number of facilitators can help you incorporate telemedicine into your organization's practice.

HealthMedia

Ann Arbor, Michigan–based HealthMedia (www.healthmedia.com) offers providers, insurers, and employers digital health coaching for their employees and members. Coaches work online with patients to provide each patient a consultation, an individualized plan, and follow-up check-ins. Patients can access an array of online tools and smartphone applications, including weight trackers, exercise logs, and health data records such as blood pressure and cholesterol reports. The HealthMedia system is designed to treat disease, foster prevention, and encourage patient compliance and follow-up.

Each patient receives a personalized plan that adheres to tested clinical and behavioral change guidelines. The system encourages and motivates the patient to follow his action plan, take his medications, and stay confident in the process and his own ability to participate.

ZigBee Health Care

ZigBee is a set of technical standards for wireless communication, comparable to a simpler, less expensive Bluetooth that specializes in monitoring and control devices.

ZigBee Health Care (www.zigbee.org/healthcare) based in San Ramon, California, provides an open standard for monitoring and management of healthcare and wellness devices. The initiative is part of the ZigBee Alliance, an association of companies working together to provide wireless solutions for monitoring and control devices. The ZigBee Alliance collaborates with the American Telemedicine Association to promote the technology to providers and consumers.

HOT TIPS AND INSIGHTS

- The typical American family is predisposed to telemedicine: it already spends more money annually to stay wired than it does on automobile gasoline.
- Mobile technology lets patients keep in touch with doctors and nurses using voice, text, and pictures; store their personal health information; and transmit data about their current health.
- Providers who use telemedicine have found that the cost per patient has declined while overall revenues have increased.
- Telemedicine facilitators can help you lay a foundation for telemedicine.

CHAPTER 7

Globalization

IN THIS CHAPTER:

- Global medical tourism
- Regional medical tourism
- Partnerships, affiliations, and geographic expansion

JUST AS THE INVENTION of the telephone changed communication forever, the Internet is transforming knowledge into a commodity and setting the stage for global and regional medical tourism.

Global medical tourism is the practice of traveling to another country for surgical, medical, or dental care. Patients seek care abroad to save money, avoid long waits, or access services unavailable at home.

Who has a stake in global medical tourism? Insurance administrators and agents, airlines, employers, top domestic and international hospitals, hotel chains, departments of tourism and ministries of health, technology and software companies, public and private hospitals, health and medical resorts and spas, travel agencies, health consulting companies, health and medical associations, medical travel agencies, property developers, international insurance companies, technology solutions providers, and, perhaps most important to hospital executives, U.S. employers.

THE RISKS AND REWARDS OF GLOBAL MEDICAL TOURISM

Language barriers, cultural issues, and traveling itself add risk to medical tourism. Long airplane flights pose the risk of embolism and other complications. Other risks are exposure to infectious diseases, limited opportunities for follow-up care, traveling too soon after surgery, and less effective recourse should things go wrong. Some medical conditions do not lend themselves to medical tourism. For example, attempting to treat chronic disease in a concentrated period often proves ineffective.

The emerging picture is that medical tourism does provide the benefits that many patients seek, including first-class accommodations, expert care, lower cost, and high satisfaction.

An Industry on the Upswing

India, Singapore, South Africa, and the United States already have strong footholds in the medical tourism market. In 2005 approximately 150,000 people visited India for medical treatment, and Malaysia hosted 375,000 medical tourists in 2008. Indian authorities expect this volume to continue to grow (Odiabat 2010; Chinai and Goswami 2007).

Most medical tourists find that providers' communication and the quality of treatment are excellent. Overall, the services are as good as or better than they would receive in the United States. The cost for most procedures, even with airfare and two weeks' hotel stay for recovery time, are 50 to 80 percent less than similar procedures performed in the United States (MedRetreat 2010).

A heart bypass procedure in Thailand costs $11,000, versus $130,000 in the United States. At $13,000, knee replacement surgery in Singapore costs far less than the U.S. rate, $40,000. However, many medical tourists do come to the United States to seek services that they cannot obtain at home (AMA-OMSS 2007).

Willing and Able

In one poll, 40 percent of surveyed U.S. healthcare consumers responded that they would be willing to travel overseas for healthcare if faced with an expensive health issue (Deloitte 2008). American hospitals may lose $160 billion annually to medical tourism (*Economist* 2008). Some U.S. insurance companies have incorporated foreign healthcare into their overall coverage and offer discounts to customers who travel overseas.

The Deloitte Center for Health Solutions (2008) projects that by 2012, an estimated 1.6 million Americans will combine foreign vacations with medical procedures. Most such incidents of medical tourism will be for short-stay outpatient procedures such as dental crowns, Lasik, or carpal tunnel surgery, at an average cost of 30 to 70 percent less than in the United States

The trend is driven by the development of companies that market and facilitate medical tourism; increases in individual insurance policies, particularly those with high deductibles; and greater insurance coverage for international medical care.

Accreditation to Ensure Quality Care

To find a trustworthy provider in the complex medical tourism world, consumers look for accredited organizations. Groups offering accreditation and safety assurances for medical tourists include the Joint Commission, the Medical Tourism Association (MTA), the Alliance for Patient Safety, HealthCare Tourism International,

Joint Commission International, and the International Medical Travel Association.

The Medical Tourism Association

The MTA's Medical Tourism Facilitator Certification program gives recipients many benefits over those who do not have certification. The MTA's Quality of Care Project aims for transparency by standardizing reporting methods of quality of care data. Patients, employers, and insurance companies can easily compare the patient safety, patient volume, costs, and quality of care of top international hospitals and healthcare facilities. The MTA also publishes *Medical Tourism Magazine*, a monthly trade journal.

Implications for Your Hospital

The medical tourism industry is destined to be among the world's major growth industries. What can you do to remain competitive?

- Consider becoming an actively involved MTA member.
- Compare the risk-adjusted results of your facility and physicians with those of the best hospitals located anywhere on the globe. Consumers can make the same comparisons. Do you stand out favorably?
- Seek relationships with international, national, and regional hospitals to learn what it takes to meet the highest standards of value.

THE MEDICAL TOURISM CONGRESS

The annual World Medical Tourism and Global Healthcare Congress is a chance for more than 2,000 healthcare executives, medical tourism facilitators, self-funded health plan directors, government agencies, and clinic and medical healthcare administrators to share knowledge and network. The congress held its first meeting in 2008.

LEADING GLOBAL MEDICAL TOURISM ENTERPRISES

The Medical Tourism Corporation, Healthbase, and HealthGlobe are standout enterprises. Your organization can learn from their operations, programs, and plans.

The Medical Tourism Corporation

The Medical Tourism Corporation (MTC) (www.medicaltourism co.com) is an international medical travel firm that helps tourists get cosmetic, dental, and medical procedures. MTC specializes in tourism to India, Mexico, Costa Rica, and Thailand. The company targets uninsured, underinsured, and cost-conscious patients. MTC's network hospitals offers savings of 40 to 80 percent off of U.S. prices. Hip resurfacing ($55,000 in the United States) could cost only $8,000 through MTC's network, and a knee surgery in India would cost about $7,000, compared to $48,000 in the United States.

Visitors to MTC's website can receive a free estimate for up to four procedures by filling out a brief online form. MTC offers almost 200 procedures in 19 service lines.

Planning is key to a successful medical tourism venture. MTC handles travel arrangements, including transporting the customer in the destination country; finds discounts on airfare, ground transportation, car rentals, lodging, and other expenses; and ensures hospitals don't have hidden fees. Customers get passport and visa assistance, direct pretravel consultations with providers, and an onsite agent who handles all needs during the visit and ensures a comfortable stay.

MTC also provides a mobile phone and Internet access so customers can stay connected to home. On returning to the United States, customers engage in a post-discharge phone consultation.

Implications for Your Hospital

As transparency prevails globally and core measures become requisite, anyone can quickly find highly accurate, relevant comparison information.

- How does the transparency movement make you view your facility and your product/service mix differently?
- What does your hospital need to do now to adapt to global competition?
- What needs to change for your facility to stay competitive?
- Are you willing to brainstorm about new possibilities that were out of the question in years past?
- Will you contemplate partnerships, affiliations, and joint strategies?
- Can you abandon sacred cows in favor of cash cows?

Healthbase

Healthbase (www.healthbase.com) connects its customers with leading healthcare facilities around the world. The company arranges an array of medical tourism services, from initial consultations to intricate surgical procedures and full service treatments in overseas hospitals.

Healthbase works with a network of internationally accredited hospitals and health clinics in Belgium, Hungary, Costa Rica, Brazil, Mexico, Panama, Thailand, Singapore, the Philippines,

Malaysia, South Korea, Turkey, and India. The company plans to extend partnerships into New Zealand, Australia, El Salvador, Argentina, Guatemala, Taiwan, Jordan, the United Kingdom, and Canada.

Healthbase continually reevaluates partners through research, on-site visits, and patient feedback. All network hospitals are screened for quality of care, pricing, procedural availability, and overall patient care.

Prospective customers can have their medical records transferred quickly to the hospitals of choice and receive a cost estimate within two or three business days. Then, with Healthbase's online portal, consumers can arrange their trips from start to finish.

Healthbase's global network offers more than 200 medical procedures, 500 ICU units, 2,000 doctors, and 8,000 beds. The data they provide is visitor-friendly; users can click on the names of network hospitals and surgeons and receive instant profiles.

Surgical services though Healthbase network hospitals represent a 60 to 80 percent savings over prevailing rates in the United States, not including travel expenses. Hip resurfacing (U.S. cost: $55,000) can be done in Singapore for $14,000, Thailand for $10,000, or India for $7,000. A facelift ($20,000 in the United States) costs $6,000, $5,000, and $3,000 in Singapore, Thailand, and India, respectively.

Implications for Your Hospital

You can't compete with the vast array of facilities available to the medical tourist. What lessons can you draw, however, from operations such as Healthbase and the customers they have successfully served?

- Is your website all it could be?
- Does your website offer comprehensive and current information about your facilities, doctors, and procedures?

- Does the site provide patient testimonials and memoirs?
- Have you collected and posted case histories?
- Do you have inspirational pictures and personal histories online?

As competition for customers grows, expand your options.

HealthGlobe

Boston-based HealthGlobe (www.myhealthglobe.com) facilitates medical tourism for individual patients and corporations. Formerly called Patient Without Borders, HealthGlobe works with the highest quality hospitals worldwide to provide 24 kinds of surgery. HealthGlobe works with businesses and insurers in its corporate medical travel division and helps educate employees of those companies about the benefits of medical travel.

HealthGlobe coordinates travel arrangements through their approved partnerships, accommodates the needs of each customer, offers 24-hour concierge and translation services at the destination, and arranges referrals for preoperative and postoperative care including coordinated support with personal nurses, physical therapists, and occupational therapists. Each patient is assigned a HealthGlobe Patient Advocate who organizes the case and accompanies the patient from initial planning through recovery.

Myhealthglobe.com provides news releases and articles and aggregates news from other sources to reassure patients and outline industry trends. The site also offers patient testimonials and a frequently asked questions section detailing partner hospitals and surgical procedures. The company's blog (http://blog.myhealthglobe .com) provides simple, engaging analysis of medical travel trends and issues. HealthGlobe is social media savvy, with presences on Twitter, Facebook, LinkedIn, and YouTube.

Implications for Your Hospital

Does your hospital attract prospective customers, particularly those with a need for high-ticket surgical procedures, using narratives that appeal to their emotions?

- Is your message too matter-of-fact? Keep in mind that prospective patients may be unsure and frightened of their medical future.
- Have you reviewed your online and print literature for its emotional appeal?
- Do you talk about the success of previous patients?
- Do you offer encouragement, hope, and inspiration?
- You may have the facts and the figures, but do you have the empathy?

Have you identified opportunities to recast the narrative of your services? It's worth a department-by-department, top-down and back-again review.

- Do you provide Q&A-style articles?
- Do you offer frequently asked questions, special reports, and fact sheets?
- Does your literature put people at ease about using your services?
- What can patients expect?
- What clinical outcomes are likely?
- How will patients feel in your care?

More medical tourism facilitators enter the industry all the time, each offering something new or different. Worldwide transparency is inevitable. The progressive institutions will thrive, the merely excellent will survive, and the ordinary will perish.

AFFILIATION AND PARTNERSHIP

If you can't fight global competitors, join or affiliate with them. Cleveland Clinic's global expansion strategy is a prime example of a U.S. provider going global. Cleveland Clinic has forged partnerships in Austria, Egypt, and the United Arab Emirates and has considered expanding to China and other markets (Cleveland Clinic 2010; Dar Al Fouad 2010; Seper 2008). The clinic manages and operates Sheikh Khalifa Medical City, a network of facilities in Abu Dhabi. Starting in 2012, the clinic will operate Cleveland Clinic Abu Dhabi.

Johns Hopkins began its global venture in 2000 in Singapore with what is now called Johns Hopkins Singapore International Medical Centre (Johns Hopkins 2009). The 30-bed licensed oncology facility is accredited by the Joint Commission and is part of the international research collaboration Cancer Therapeutics Research Group.

The Harvard Medical School Dubai Center Institute for Postgraduate Education and Research was launched in 2004 through a joint effort by Partners Harvard Medical International and Dubai Healthcare City. The facility is part of the Dubai government's mission to develop Dubai Healthcare City into a center of excellence for healthcare delivery, medical education, and research. In return for lending its knowledge and the brand, Harvard earns revenue, increases its brand globally, and influences the next generation of medical students (HMSDC 2007).

Implications for Your Hospital

Have you explored opportunities to affiliate around the globe?

- Where can you establish brand recognition, gain revenue, and influence students to intern at your hospital?

- Are you completely transparent and competitive in price and quality? Can you adapt your cost structures and mix of services to the new marketplace?

INDIA'S ASSEMBLY-LINE SURGERY

In Bangalore, India, Narayana Hrudayalaya Health City uses economies of scale to drive down the cost of healthcare. The *Wall Street Journal* dubbed founder Devi Shetty the Henry Ford of heart surgery for his transformational factory model of healthcare (Anand 2009).

The health city offers leading-edge medical care at a fraction of the costs found elsewhere in the world. The flagship hospital, Narayana Hrudayalaya Heart Hospital, charges an average of $2,000 for open-heart surgery, compared to $20,000 to $100,000 in U.S. hospitals (Anand 2009).

The simple driving force behind this low cost of care is volume. Just as Toyota revolutionized manufacturing, Shetty has systemized medical procedures, even as intricate, sophisticated, and potentially hazardous as heart surgery. The heart hospital is a 1,000-bed facility where surgeons safely operate at an unheard-of pace—42 cardiac surgeons completing 3,174 cardiac bypass surgeries in 2008, more than double Cleveland Clinic's 1,367 surgeries that year.

The hospital achieves economies of scale by employing equipment three to four more times per day than the typical U.S. hospital does. Surgeons perform two or three procedures a day, six days a week, working a total of 60 to 70 hours per week. U.S. surgeons work fewer than 60 hours and perform one or two surgeries a day, five days a week. To prevent fatigue, Shetty's surgeons take breaks after three or four hours in surgery (Anand 2009).

Some question whether Shetty's model poses a risk to quality. However, success rates are comparable to other hospitals abroad.

Profitable and Growing

Shetty's business group makes a larger-than-average profit: 7.7 percent after taxes, slightly greater than U.S. hospitals' 6.9 percent average (AHA 2008). Expansion plans are in the works, and Dr. Shetty hopes to increase the number of systemwide hospital beds to 30,000. This expansion would make it the largest private-pay hospital group in the nation. At that size, the group could purchase directly from suppliers, bypassing traditional medical equipment sales channels.

Narayana Hrudayalaya Health City offers some lessons: As you specialize, your performance and efficiency improve. Correct management can decrease the cost per procedure. Theoretically, U.S. hospitals could also achieve these economies of scale.

Implications for Your Hospital

Even if they're located next door to you, U.S. employers have no qualms about partnering with hospitals in Thailand or India. Every procedure you offer is subject to intense competition. Now is the time to consider new ideas.

Despite entrenched bureaucracy, overregulation, and fixed costs, opportunities abound. Be willing to look with new eyes. Challenge existing norms, procedures, and organizational cultures. Changing will be difficult, and you will face disagreements along the way. But the alternatives—reduced volumes, loss of high margin procedures—are more problematic than the pain of changing.

REGIONAL TOURISM

Medical tourism within the United States, which we'll call regional tourism, is increasing at a significant pace. Before regional medical tourism became an option, most Americans who needed complicated medical procedures sought treatment in their hometown hospitals. Today's consumers want more command over their personal healthcare and do whatever is necessary to get the care at the best price.

Sometimes consumers leave home even when local facilities can treat their medical issue, if local care is unsatisfactory. When treatment for diabetes and kidney failure wasn't working at her Chicago hospital and her heart began to fail, one Chicago resident sought care from the Mayo Clinic in Rochester, Minnesota. Mayo Clinic solved her problem by changing her medications. Further care at Mayo saved the patient's feet and one of her hands after Illinois hospitals had recommended amputation (Boodman 2009).

Today's proactive patients research the most promising treatment for their conditions. One Seattle executive was diagnosed with a massive benign brain tumor and was hopeful about a procedure at the University of Pittsburgh Medical Center (UPMC). Though his local neurosurgeon doubted the benefits of traveling to Pittsburgh for the procedure, the executive was undaunted. He spoke to UPMC's head surgeon, studied the data from the procedure, and compared UPMC's results to those of local neurosurgeons. He decided that the procedure in Pittsburgh would be his best option, but his insurance company balked at his request. When the executive obtained a letter from the head surgeon in Pittsburgh detailing the prospects for a shorter and less expensive hospital stay, a quicker recovery, and reduction of post-operative risk, the insurance company approved the plan. The treatment was successful (Boodman 2009).

How Patients Select Destinations

The would-be regional tourist has much to consider before deciding where to receive care, even when the data and anecdotal evidence are compelling. The traveler has to consider the cost of travel itself and to what extent her insurance covers the procedure. She must also consider the benefits of being in familiar surroundings and proximity to family and friends, plus options for extended stay if necessary. Smart consumers also want to know how often the destination hospital has treated other patients with the same condition.

As transparency becomes the norm, consumers can make comparisons based on experience, quality, and price. They make lists, narrow their options based on research, and may make the decision to have their procedure done halfway across the country. Patients make comparisons through articles discussing the hospital's care, through *U.S.News and World Report* rankings, and from other independent sources.

Websites like Hospital Compare (www.hospitalcompare.hhs .gov; see Chapter 1) and Consumers' Checkbook (www.checkbook .org) may spur the growth of regional tourism.

Furthermore, quality matters more than cost in most consumers' decisions to travel for care (Gillentine 2008). With their health at stake, consumers go wherever they have to. As more customers get HSAs and consumer-driven health plans and can seek healthcare anywhere, regional tourism will rise.

Implications for Your Hospital

It's hard to know just how many consumers engage in regional medical tourism. As opposed to global medical tourism, which generally involves a facilitator, regional medical tourists are more likely to research and plan on their own.

You may have regional tourists already. Do you have a system that tracks where patients are coming from?

INSURANCE AND REGIONAL TOURISM

Insurance providers are generally unwilling to cover travel expenses and may not be keen on having members travel out of state for treatment except for serious, rare, or complex medical issues. However, insurance companies are increasingly willing to participate if patients' use of specialty hospitals or out-of-state facilities saves the insurers money. Some insurance providers are even making regional tourism an attractive option.

The BlueCard network lets members of one Blue Cross and Blue Shield branch get services anywhere in the United States. The Care Comparison tool lets patients compare costs at different network hospitals.

At www.uhc.com/find_a_physician.htm, members of United Healthcare can research the plan's 4,600 network hospitals and 560,000 network doctors. Site visitors can get quality, cost, and procedure-specific information about providers across the country. Members may choose regional medical tourism based on the findings and, depending on their particular insurance plan, may be covered for out-of-state services.

STRATEGIES FOR TAPPING REGIONAL MEDICAL TOURISM

Become a Center of Excellence

Some U.S. medical facilities try to fight international medical tourism by becoming domestic or international medical destinations themselves. Being regarded as a center of excellence widens a hospital's appeal and may result in business from insurance companies that encourage members with rare or complex conditions to travel to such centers. Treatment centers of excellence can afford patients a better outlook, and traveling regionally rather than internationally gives them ease of care and coordination between their local physician and destination surgeon.

In Orlando, Florida, the Lake Nona Science and Technology Park is a 600-acre medical city. When complete, the medical city will include the University of Central Florida's College of Medicine and

Healthcare Campus, Sanford-Burnham Medical Research Institute at Lake Nona, MD Anderson Cancer Center Orlando, Nemours Children's Hospital Orlando, Orlando VA Medical Center, and University of Florida Academic and Research Center. The medical city promotes itself as a medical tourism destination.

MD Anderson Cancer Center has a site in the Orlando medical city and is based in Houston, Texas. The center's vision is to be the world's premiere cancer center, and it has positioned itself as a medical destination. In 2008, of the 79,000-plus patients treated at the center, more than 11 percent were from outside the immediate area (Dolan 2008).

To establish your facility as a medical destination, you must have a niche. Highly specialized and concentrated experience in certain procedures is a compelling feature; affordable price is another. The combination of the two would be a spectacular draw. Start by deciding which one or two aspects of your care you'll promote. Then comes the hard task of marketing what you have to offer.

Bring Care to Patients Through Geographic Expansion

Some U.S. hospitals have established facilities in multiple states, expanding domestically as a variation on regional tourism.

Headquartered in Rochester, Minnesota, Mayo Clinic also has campuses in Jacksonville, Florida, and Scottsdale/Phoenix, Arizona. Mayo Health System operates hospitals and clinics in 70 communities in Minnesota, Iowa, and Wisconsin, pairing Mayo expertise with local care.

Ohio-based Cleveland Clinic has facilities in Florida and Las Vegas in addition to its international Canada and Abu Dhabi offerings. The clinic's reach has also expanded geographically by offering its services within existing hospital facilities.

For example, Rochester Heart Institute at Rochester General Hospital in New York is a Cleveland Clinic Heart Surgery Center. Surgeons use Cleveland Clinic's standards and Rochester physicians benefit from the shared expertise. Rochester owns the facilities and provides supporting services. The clinic has other heart surgery affiliates in Illinois, North Carolina, Pennsylvania, and South Carolina.

Price Competitively

Sometimes the cost structure of a particular hospital is favorable to would-be regional tourists and makes the destination attractive. When a hospital has the latest technology, it might perform a procedure more cost-effectively than hospitals without that technology.

Some hospitals encourage regional tourism by charging a single, up-front price that is negotiated beforehand. This can range from 50 to 75 percent less than the consumer might pay if treated at home. Why would a U.S. hospital or health clinic be willing to receive far less compensation?

For one, they avoid altogether the unpleasant task of seeking reimbursement from third-party administrators or insurers after the procedure. Also, when the fee is paid up front, a whole host of accounting and administrative procedures, in themselves costly, are bypassed entirely.

Some hospitals actively compete for the medical tourism market, luring customers who might otherwise travel overseas. The Canadian company North American Surgery connects patients in North America with U.S. hospitals that are willing to compete on price with providers across the state, throughout the country, and around the globe.

California-based chiropractor Thomas Van Buskirk had no insurance and a blocked carotid artery. The surgery in the Bay Area would have cost about $70,000. To have the surgery in India, including travel expenses and an extended stay, would have cost only $12,000. Buskirk, with North American Surgery's help, found the Oklahoma Heart Hospital, which did the surgery for $15,000 (*Kiplinger's* 2009).

Meet Employers' Needs

Some employers leverage prices they've arranged with foreign hospitals to secure attractive rates with domestic hospitals. Some U.S. hospitals capitulate, offering attractive deals to employers when the possibility of volume business is involved.

In 2008, Hannaford Brothers, a supermarket chain based in Scarborough, Maine, publicly announced that employees requiring knee and hip replacements would be sent to Singapore to save the company money. Hip replacement in the United States would cost about $43,000, but only $9,000 in Singapore. To gain business, several Maine hospitals put in bids to match that much lower price (Huang 2009).

Employers are conscious of the time frames required to send employees overseas for care and the cost of that lost time. Accordingly, working with domestic hospitals for volume business is attractive. Saving on healthcare is so appealing that some employers incentivize their employees to seek regional healthcare tourism—through waiving deductibles, giving wellness credits, lowering deductibles or copayments, and providing travel allowances to employees and their companions.

With volume business, your hospital receives compensation up front, and it comes in the form of a single lump-sum payment negotiated in advance. This scenario is a triple-win. The employer saves money, employees are treated effectively, and your hospital receives the fee.

Make Medical Tourists Feel at Home

Easy accommodations make a hospital a more appealing regional tourism destination. Hospitals and clinics are building guest houses and partnering with hotels to provide medical tourists and their families with convenient lodging during the procedure and recovery.

Penrose Hospital in Colorado Springs opened the John Zay Guest House in 2008, a facility with 11 suites, wireless Internet, and a full kitchen. MD Anderson Cancer Center's Houston operation owns the Jesse H. Jones Rotary House International, a hotel operated by Marriott that is connected to the center by a walkway.

Cleveland Clinic offers a medical concierge services that arranges lodging, air and ground transportation, and interpreter services for its nonlocal patients. The Seattle Cancer Care Alliance runs SCCA House, an 80-unit extended stay facility built with its patients in mind—the environment is clean and carefully monitored to protect the health of its many immunosuppressed patients.

Implications for Your Hospital

Opportunities to attract patients by upgrading your facilities may be well within your grasp.

- Can you purchase local facilities and convert them into guest houses or hotels? If you can't make a purchase, can you form an alliance or affiliation?
- Are there facilities on your own premises that might serve well to house medical tourists?
- What else in your immediate area can heighten the notion that your hospital is a valid and worthy medical destination?

REGIONAL MEDICAL TOURISM FACILITATORS

A new breed of vendor facilitates regional tourism to the benefit of employers and domestic hospitals. These companies work with high-ranking hospitals to give patients quality care outside their home regions.

BridgeHealth Medical (www.bridgehealthmedical.com) negotiates rates with U.S. hospitals to provide lower-priced medical procedures. The company first facilitated global medical tourism, through BridgeHealth International.

Healthplace America (www.healthplaceamerica.com), based in Lisle, Illinois, is devoted solely to regional tourism for surgery. The network can provide employers with savings of between 30 and 50 percent over rates negotiated by insurers when the employer pays up front in cash.

Healthcare Concierge Services' HCS Navigator (http://hcsnavigator.com) provides administrative services and case management along with the travel and lodging logistics arranged by other facilitators.

Implications for Your Hospital

Perhaps it is time to establish an in-house office to identify, contact, and negotiate with area employers directly, and to establish your own fixed per-case rate for volume business. Particularly for employers who self-insure, overtures from your facility could be welcome.

HERE TO STAY

Global and regional medical tourism is not going to disappear. If anything, the phenomenon will prove to be a spectacular growth industry. Taking advantage of opportunities to redirect your course now is likely to be easier than trying to play catch-up later.

Don't try to be all things to all people. Let prospective patients know where you excel. The more of something you do, the better you become at it. Strengthen and accentuate your strong points.

Creativity, ingenuity, and new arrangements and relationships offer solutions to dilemmas that before seemed unsolvable. In this age of hyperintense competition from all corners, it is possible to run a profitable hospital. The future belongs to hospitals and healthcare executives who engage in bold, innovative, and aggressive thinking. Fortunately, no one has a monopoly on that.

HOT TIPS AND INSIGHTS

- Medical tourism, especially from the United States, is driven by costs, the absence of local services, and excessive wait times for a procedure.
- Anyone anywhere can quickly find highly accurate, relevant healthcare comparison information as transparency and core measures prevail globally.
- Leading-edge medical care at low rates happens when the volume of business is high, the provider's experience is vast, and the procedures are monitored effectively.
- A new breed of innovative and aggressive vendors is facilitating regional tourism to the benefit of employers and domestic hospitals.
- Creativity, ingenuity, and new partnerships offer potential solutions to hyperintense global competition.

CHAPTER 8

Social Media

IN THIS CHAPTER:

- Social media grows dominant
- Hospitals signing on
- Real-time information and updates
- Creating online communities

HOSPITALS AND HEALTHCARE institutions are embracing social media at a rapid pace and are using it in a variety of ways. An August 28, 2010, report showed that 825 hospitals were actively employing social media on a daily or weekly basis. Of those 825 hospitals, 634 maintained Twitter accounts, 631 had Facebook pages, 391 had a YouTube channel, and 87 had blogs (Bennett 2010). It is imperative that you include social sites in your marketing and advertising strategies and community outreach efforts.

TO YOUR FUTURE PATIENTS, SOCIAL MEDIA ARE A MUST

The patients who will account for your hospital's revenues far into the future are reaching early adulthood in an era in which Facebook and other social media dominate information gathering and exchange. This generation cannot conceive of a time when communication and the exchange of information were not primarily facilitated by social media.

A Kaiser Family Foundation study found that children aged 8 to 18 devote more than seven and a half hours daily to communication devices such as smartphones, computers, television, and other electronic devices. Many of these children use more than one medium at a time, packing almost 11 hours of media content into that seven and a half hours (Rideout, Foehr, and Roberts 2010).

Among kids aged 18 to 22—today's college students—Facebook and other social networking sites and various forms of electronic messaging are the preferred methods of discourse. Newspaper circulation is dropping everywhere. More people of all ages are going online for their news, social interaction, and through-the-grapevine information exchanges.

Even Congress uses social media—as of June 2010, 204 members (38 percent) had Twitter accounts (Zuckerman 2010). Soon, organizations that are out of the social media loop will seem antiquated.

A 2009 study by Ad-ology Research found that almost two out of five patients of hospitals and urgent care centers are influenced by hospitals' use of social media and marketing. More than half of respondents aged 25 to 34 reported being influenced by social media.

On the Front Lines

Using social media shows consumers that you speak their language. Hospitals that use Facebook, Twitter, YouTube, and blogs in a coordinated effort have gained more patients. Social media channels can be used for marketing, introducing new services, surveying and polling, and identifying new hires—today's insightful commenter could be tomorrow's new social media advisor.

A FULL EMBRACE OF SOCIAL MEDIA

Through the end of 2009, hospitals using YouTube offered more than 5,000 videos collectively and those using Twitter posted more than 10,000 tweets, according to data from the Hospital Social Network List (http://ebennett.org/hsnl).

Your customers are increasingly obtaining health information from social media sites. Adults aged 18 to 49 are most likely to participate in social media sites related to health (Fox and Jones 2009). One in four urgent care patients report being influenced by social media, and more than 40 percent of all online users have read consumer commentary about personal health, medical health, or related experiences on a website, online newsgroup, or blog (Ad-ology Research 2009).

Social media users bookmark appropriate health content, send health and medical videos to friends, post reviews of hospitals and of individual doctors, and post comments on health blogs. Social networking sites give patients, families, friends, and the general public a place in operating rooms, sometimes sharing medical procedures step by step. Real-time updates and video diminish fear and anxiety about complex medical operations. Such transmissions also inform people about the intricacies of procedures. Texting or tweeting, with proper regard paid to patient confidentiality, can update family members during their loved one's surgery.

Social media helps keep you present in community members' minds as a trusted health resource. In addition to sharing news and gaining and retaining clients, hospitals and health organizations are using social media in creative ways:

- Keeping in touch from afar. Saint Francis Hospital based in Wilmington, Delaware, sent 45 staff members on a medical mission to Peru. The hospital's Facebook page (www.facebook.com/pages/St-Francis-Hospital-Wilmington-DE/121492863345) offered postings about and pictures of the trip to publicize the hospital's work (Bothum 2009).

- Communicating in emergencies. When Saints Mary and Elizabeth Hospital in Louisville, Kentucky, experienced sustained flooding in August 2009, Facebook and Twitter were effective tools for keeping employees and customers informed and updated about the situation (see their health network's sites, www.facebook.com/jewishhospital and http://twitter.com/jewishhospital) (Wallask 2009).
- Spreading health truth and quashing rumors. During 2009's H1N1 outbreak many parents mistakenly believed that exposing their children to people who had the virus would keep the kids from getting sick. The U.S. Department of Health and Human Services, through its Facebook page and other social media outlets, formally debunked the practice (www.facebook.com/CDC; http://twitter.com/CDCgov).

ISSUES IN SOCIAL MEDIA AND HEALTHCARE

Guarding patients' privacy is an obvious and crucial part of using social media. Permission for using patients' images and information must be gained in advance. Videos of surgery must not show patients in a way that makes them recognizable to others. Great care must be taken throughout the filming to focus on the immediate area related to the procedure.

Some people ask whether or not the use of social media is consistent with the Hippocratic Oath. Take care to ensure that the use of technology doesn't supersede patient-first care.

TWITTER WHILE YOU WORK

Twitter (www.twitter.com) allows you to stay in touch with others through tweets (posts limited to 140 characters) that essentially announce, "Here's what we're up to." Hospitals use Twitter to make announcements about hospital activities, relay hospital news, and offer national health information.

Twitter allows you to attach a link within your tweet. That link can go to your website, your blog, a specific marketing campaign such as men's health awareness and immunization programs, a community service message, a news site—whatever you choose. Often these links are presented in abbreviated form using Tinyurl .com, Snipurl.com, or BitURL.net, services that truncate a cumbersome URL to one that is succinct and memorable, so you can spend more of your 140 characters relaying the important message.

You can also sign up to follow other accounts. Following competing hospitals lets you see what they are promoting, and how.

People who follow you can respond to your tweets or retweet them through their own accounts, spreading your message.

Here are some ideas for tweets and the purpose each serves:

- Highlight your medical center's (YMC) staff and organizational achievements: "YMC named one of the top 10 U.S. heart hospitals! *[link to press release on YMC site or the listmaker's site]*"
- Share health news: "American Cancer Society finds link between larger waists and higher risks of death. *[link to ACS brief]*"
- Promote events and services: "Join us at our free health fair on November 2 from 10 to 3 in Room B." (Send several tweets about each event, from far in advance to the day it occurs.)
- Create human interest and attract employees: "RN Oliver Seidler explains why he loves working at YMC. *[link to interview on hospital site or blog]*"
- Support public health and safety: "Autumn is here; don't forget to get your flu shot!"
- Publicize media appearances: "YMC's Linda Jackson, MD, talks about cancer screening on Channel 5 news. *[link to video on Channel 5 site or embedded on hospital site]*"

Review other hospitals' Twitter feeds to see what the industry is doing. Here are some exemplary Twitter accounts:

- The George Washington University Medical Center (Washington, DC): http://twitter.com/GWMedicalCenter
- LifeBridge Health (Baltimore): http://twitter.com/lbhealth
- Duncan Regional Hospital (Duncan, Oklahoma): http://twitter.com/duncanregional
- Bone and Joint Hospital at St. Anthony (Oklahoma City): http://twitter.com/boneandjointokc

Each announcement, activity, event, public service reminder, or reference source provided is another way of saying to the community, "Here we are: we are ready to serve you, we are involved, and you can trust us. See us when you're in need."

Implications for Your Hospital

If you're not already on Twitter and tweeting on a regular basis, it's time to get in the game. For the coming generation of healthcare consumers, social media is part of everyday life.

- Does your hospital have a Twitter account, and if so, are your tweets frequent, timely, and information-rich?
- Do you have a Twitter manager who is constantly seeking new developments within the hospital and items to post?
- Does this manager respond to followers' queries and comments?
- Are you encouraging your hospital community to follow you on Twitter?
- Do you have monitoring capabilities in place? When you issue a tweet do you keep tabs on how effective it is—the responses

you receive or the number of people who come to an event that you promoted through tweets?

- Do you have plenty of ideas for future tweets?
- Do you follow competing area hospitals on Twitter?

GET FRIENDLY WITH FACEBOOK

The social networking giant Facebook (www.facebook.com) has grown far beyond its original model of college students getting to know each other. Many businesses use Facebook to connect with their clients.

Like Twitter, Facebook is useful for relaying hospital news and national health information, promoting events and causes, and driving traffic to your website.

On Facebook, users post status updates similar to tweets. The status updates appear on the user's "wall" and can be longer than tweets—up to 420 characters. People who "like" (follow) the organization can post messages to the business's wall, "like" the status messages there, and respond to other followers' wall posts, making your page a place for discussion. Your hospital can follow other groups and businesses by adding them to your Favorite Pages.

Photos can be posted on your own or another's wall or in albums. Many widgets and applications are available; your hospital could show a countdown to a major event or a tally of funds raised. Users can also create, publicize, and send invitations to events.

Users can buy ads that appear on the Facebook pages of consumers in their target market. Some businesses sell items on their page through a Shop tab—you can even set up your Facebook account so it defaults to your shopping tab.

The sample tweets shared earlier can easily be adapted into Facebook status updates that promote your organization and provide information to your community. To expand your social media presence and avoid having to write duplicate information, you can link your Twitter and Facebook accounts through www.twitter.com/widgets/facebook and have Facebook update Twitter or vice-versa. You can also add a tab that links to your YouTube channel.

Here are some hospital Facebook pages worth visiting:

- Lowell General Hospital (Lowell, Massachusetts): www.facebook.com/LowellGeneralHosp
- Yale-New Haven Hospital (New Haven, Connecticut): www.facebook.com/yalenewhavenhospital
- St. Jude's Children's Research Hospital (Memphis): www.facebook.com/stjude

Implications for Your Hospital

You want to be a leader in offering information that today's social media–focused healthcare consumers share, retain, and act upon. What steps are you taking to let Facebook help?

- Does your hospital have a Facebook page, and if so, is it current, dynamic, and full of great information?
- Do you have a Facebook page manager who is constantly seeking new items to post?
- Does this manager respond to followers' posts and questions?
- Are you encouraging your hospital community to visit your Facebook page and post a comment or offer a picture? This helps position your hospital as popular, dynamic, and authoritative.
- Are you using Facebook's targeted advertising to reach your audience?

TIME TO GET LINKEDIN

LinkedIn (www.LinkedIn.com) is primarily devoted to business and career networking. Someone joins LinkedIn almost every second.

Individual users make a profile that details their current and former employers, job titles, and duties; educational history; and contact information. Members connect with past and present colleagues, business associates, clients, and schoolmates. Users can join groups and associations related to their industry, school, and interests. People who are connected may write recommendations for each other, which are also posted on the profile page. Users indicate what kind of contact they seek—career opportunities, consulting offers, staying in touch, and more. The site has a powerful job search engine.

Companies can build their own LinkedIn pages. The profile includes an overview of the organization, in which many hospitals present their corporate history and future ambitions. You can enter your hospital's specialties using linked search terms. You can also add a news box to link stories about your organization.

All business profiles offer basic contact information including specific websites, phone numbers, and addresses. LinkedIn aggregates and displays company data such as size of the workforce, common job titles, employee gender and median age of employees, and popular schools among staff.

LinkedIn is useful in recruiting new hires, increasing your Web presence, and connecting with potential customers. Individuals can sign up to follow companies and receive updates of their activity.

Peruse these substantial LinkedIn profiles:

- Norwalk Hospital (New York City):
  www.linkedin.com/companies/norwalk-hospital
- Children's Hospital of Los Angeles:
  www.linkedin.com/companies/childrens-hospital-los-angeles
- Johns Hopkins Hospital (Baltimore):
  www.linkedin.com/companies/johns-hopkins-hospital

- Duke University Hospital (Durham, North Carolina):
  www.linkedin.com/companies/duke-university-medical-center
- Mercy Hospital (Miami):
  www.linkedin.com/companies/mercy-hospital
- Moses Taylor Hospital (Scranton, Pennsylvania):
  www.linkedin.com/companies/moses-taylor-hospital

GO VISUAL WITH VIDEOS

Online video viewership is increasing rapidly. Media research firm Nielsen reported that in December 2009 the aggregate of unique viewers, total video streams, streams per viewer, and time per viewer increased by 13 percent over the previous December. By far the most popular video site is YouTube (www.youtube.com), with Hulu (www.hulu.com) a distant second with less than 10 percent the number of YouTube's viewers. All other video portals, such as Yahoo!, Turner Sports and Entertainment Digital Network, and MSN, command tiny shares of the viewing market.

On YouTube, your hospital can create its own channel, where you can upload videos and provide a summary of your hospital and a link to your websites. You can subdivide your channel by health specialties—a heart channel, a weight management channel, a cancer channel. Other users can subscribe to your channel and make comments. Your hospital can subscribe to others' channels.

The opportunities for your hospital to employ video are vast. Younger patients include video-watching in their daily routines, but the potential to serve older patients through use of video is more intriguing. Health videos appeal to older consumers who are homebound because of illness, live in rural areas, have trouble reading fine print, or simply prefer to be shown how to do something over reading instructions about it.

Health tips and follow-up care instructions are two areas to start with when your organization begins to make videos. Hospitals post patient success stories, animations explaining medical procedures, public service announcements, lectures about health issues, videos of surgeries, and footage of events and repost TV commercials and their doctors' TV appearances.

These YouTube channels are well done:

- Brigham and Women's Hospital (Boston): www.youtube.com/user/Brighamandwomens
- Cooper University Hospital (Camden, New Jersey): www.youtube.com/user/coopertv
- Akron Children's Hospital (Ohio): www.youtube.com/user/AkronChildrens
- St. Louis Children's: www.youtube.com/user/ChildrensHospitalStl

Online Video Libraries

A review of online health video libraries can spark ideas for your own content. HealthCentral (www.HealthCentral.com) offers an impressive array of authoritative videos about more than 35 health conditions, in addition to a variety of other health education services. Site features include a robust search engine, a health library, condition-specific in-depth reports, quizzes, calculators and other tools, and 3D medical animations. Each medical condition is explored deeply; for example, heart-related videos include "Stem Cells Reversing Heart Damage," "Medicine's Next Big Thing? Growing Hearts," "Heart Valves and Surgical Ablation," and more than 40 others.

There are more than 100 condition-specific health channels on eMedTV (www.eMedTV.com). eMedTV's content is reviewed by on-staff doctors, pharmacists, and physical therapists and is also peer-reviewed. The site offers hundreds of health videos and a vast library of text articles. The site's *HealthSavvy* e-mail digest service keeps users up to date about the medical topics of their choosing.

Health-centric video site icyou (www.icyou.com) is built much like YouTube. Hospitals, other medical organizations, doctors, and individuals can create channels, post videos, and comment on others' offerings. These channels offer interesting content:

- Medical University of South Carolina (Charleston): www.icyou.com/channel/musc-health
- Baton Rouge General: www.icyou.com/user/batonrougegeneral
- Alegent Health (Iowa and Nebraska): www.icyou.com/channel/alegenthealths-channel
- National Institutes of Health: www.icyou.com/channel/nih4healths-channel
- *Journal of the American Medical Association:* www.icyou.com/channel/jamareportvideos-channel

Implications for Your Hospital

Are you developing videos for YouTube or your website?

- Have you identified basic introductory material for video, including how-to health-related tips and follow-up care instructions?
- Have you mapped out features about your key departments, profiles of your doctors and staff, and case histories?
- What are your prospects for developing an online video library?

HOSPITALS IN THE BLOGOSPHERE

A blog, short for weblog, is an online journal. Blogs can contain the same information you might promote through Facebook or Twitter but have no word count limits. You can make announcements, introduce new products or services, profile your doctors or key professional staff, offer public service messages, hold contests, and solicit feedback in the form of comments.

Consider offering magazine-style entries about popular health topics—your doctors can write a compelling guest article, and at the article's end the doctor's bio and contact information can lead to business for your organization.

Your blog is a separate information entity that should be updated more frequently than your website. Readers can subscribe to your blog through an RSS feed or bookmark your blog to keep up with what you're posting.

Some hospitals have a separate URL for their blog—for example, www.OurHospital.com would become www.OurHospitalBlog.com. Other hospitals simply make the blog an extension of the existing URL, so www.OurHospital.com would feature its blog at www.OurHospital.com/blogname.

A simple, popular option is to set up a blog through a blogging platforms such as WordPress (http://wordpress.org) or Blogger (www.blogger.com/start).

Sherman Health (Elgin, IL) offers several blogs, including dedicated sites for patient testimonials and cardiac care, and a general blog that promotes service lines, gives community information, and shares what's new around the hospital (www.shermanhealth.com/blogs.php).

Seattle Children's Hospital offers Seattle Mama Doc (http://seattlemamadoc.seattlechildrens.org), full of well-written articles by a pediatrician who is also a mother.

Rose Knows Health (http://rosemedicalcenter.wordpress.com) is an engaging blog from Denver's Rose Medical Center. The posts blend health information that consumers demand with quotes from their doctors, emphasizing their staff's expertise while providing valuable and entertaining popular health education.

Podcasts: Audio to Go

Some hospitals offer a series of podcasts: focused audio messages ranging in length from three or four minutes to an hour or more. Blog visitors can stream podcasts from the hospital's website or blog or download them to their iPod or other mobile audio device and can subscribe through e-mail or RSS feed.

Johns Hopkins Medicine (www.hopkinsmedicine.org/mediaii/podcasts.html) offers weekly podcasts, usually running around 10 minutes each. The podcasts are subdivided into minute-long sections on the latest health news. A sample week's offering: treatment for gallstones, simpler assessment of blood lipids, moods while on low-fat or low-carb diets, and better kidney functioning. Past podcasts are archived so that anyone may click on any previous program and quickly get to the topic of his choice.

Medical University of South Carolina in Charleston (www.muschealth.com/multimedia/Podcasts/index.aspx) has a vast podcast library—almost 1,000 podcasts about nearly 40 topics. The podcasts range from 1-minute news updates to 15-minute lectures.

Henry Ford Health System in Detroit produces the Medical Minute Podcast (http://henryford.com/medicalminutepodcast). Each podcast pairs a specific topic with a health expert—"Women's Hair Loss" with a dermatologist, "Hearing Loss and Age" with an audiologist, "Diabetes Myths" with a diabetes nurse educator.

Implications for Your Hospital

For your blog to be of interest, it must be frequently updated—aim for a few posts a week. The more blog contributors you have, the easier it is to keep the blog current and viable. Consider asking several specialists to contribute their own weekly mini-blog—just 100 to 150 words per post.

Podcasting is not difficult. Most computers have a suitable recording function with which your subject matter experts can produce .wav or .mp3 sound files for direct posting on your site.

Are you ready to enter the blogosphere?

- Have you identified the issues of greatest interest to your hospital community?
- Do you know subject matter experts who can serve as hosts?
- Who among your administrative staff has the technical capabilities to get your blog up and running?
- Who can assist with podcasts and other blog elements?
- What pictures, graphics, icons, and other design elements can you borrow from your hospital's existing website?

Are you willing to wait until the competitors in your area are already fully adept at interacting with and serving the local community from their blogs? Recognize the value of initiating sooner rather than later.

ONLINE COMMUNITIES

Beyond a simple blog, online communities expand the networking aspect of social networking. A condition-specific online community has a specific target and a built-in audience. These communities feature message boards or chat rooms where patients can meet and support others with their same conditions and ask questions of health experts.

The free online community Patients Like Me (www.patients likeme.com; also detailed in Chapter 2's discussion of e-patients) lets members share their health information with one another, learning about new treatments and gaining support. Patients create a shared health profile; the data they share lets doctors and researchers see the real-world impact of treatments and can advance research.

At www.webmd.com/community/blogs, WebMD offers a blend of a blog an and online community. Health experts cover cancer treatment and care, diet and fitness, anxiety and stress management, allergies and asthma, and cholesterol management, among dozens of other topics. The interactive communities are moderated by WebMD staff. The site invites visitors to join the discussion about topics such as healthy parenting, dermatology, smoking cessation, body image, and pharmaceuticals.

WellCommunity (http://wellcommunitychicago.org), run by Swedish Covenant Hospital, is a magazine and discussion forum that is also a great marketing tool. The articles are engaging, and the local focus shows that the hospital cares about its community.

BrainTalk (http://braintalkcommunities.org/forums) is an online community of neurology patients and caregivers that was established in 1993. PsychCentral, which also offers a health library and blogs, hosts a variety of mental health–centric forums at http://forums .psychcentral.com.

Implications for Your Hospital

Who will be responsible for making your social media plans reality?

Someone in your hospital should be assigned to devote efforts to disseminating news on Twitter, Facebook, and other social media sites. This social media officer should make multiple daily, relevant posts that will influence customers and prospects in your target area.

You need to be aware of your hospital's position in the marketplace:

- What people are saying about your organization—manage your perception by addressing any negative comments found online
- What your competitors are doing
- What's happening in healthcare and hospitals

Your social media officer could spend all day visiting an array of chat rooms, forums, and commentary sites to keep abreast of the information you need. One way to save time is to set up Google Alerts. After setting up an account at www.google.com/alerts, you enter a list of the terms you would like to search for and Google sends you an e-mail digest with links to content about that subject. You choose how often you get alerts and what kind of content to receive (news, Web, blogs, videos, groups, or all of these).

The most useful phrase to set up an alert for is the name of your organization; this allows you to see what people are saying about you. Other useful terms are your doctors' names, specific medical conditions, competing hospitals' names, and industry trends (for example, you can get updates about the swine flu outbreak from Google Alerts by adding *H1N1* to your alerts list).

A GOLD MINE AWAITS

Take advantage of the fact that the United States is a marketing gold mine for the hospital that can electronically reach its patient base. Though there is growth in global and regional medical tourism, healthcare is primarily local. Twitter, Facebook, and similar sites can be great tools for mounting local community outreach campaigns.

While hospitals have employed marketing and advertising campaigns for several years and have long issued their own news releases, social media sites are so convenient, inexpensive, and accessible to all that they are irresistible as an outreach tool. Consumers experience a stronger connection to a hospital when they follow its Twitter updates or "like" its Facebook page.

HOT TIPS AND INSIGHTS

- Facebook and other social media dominate channels of information gathering and exchange.
- Because social media sites can be used to target consumers, they are rapidly becoming a primary marketing and advertising vehicle.
- Community outreach via social media can be simple, inexpensive, and highly effective.
- A hospital blog can help anyone who wants to conveniently monitor your hospital's activities and stay in touch with you.
- Developing targeted online communities is an efficient way to build interest in specific healthcare issues and position your hospital as a vital resource.

CHAPTER 9

Targeted Marketing to Consumers

IN THIS CHAPTER:

- Hospitals marketing through all media outlets
- Advocacy journalism and product placement
- Taking the higher road
- Novel approaches to marketing

THE TABOOS ABOUT healthcare providers marketing directly to patients have been subsiding for several decades. It was once unthinkable for doctors, lawyers, and other professional service providers to overtly advertise in any way. Clients, patients, and customers were attracted by word of mouth from family and friends.

As soon as appealing directly to end users became standard fare, service providers and institutions including hospitals, universities, municipalities, and places of worship jumped into it. Pharmaceutical companies that once made their pitch directly to healthcare providers, independent labs, and doctors' offices now routinely air national ads directed to consumers, offering help for erectile dysfunction, high blood pressure, high cholesterol, and dozens of other conditions.

Future healthcare marketing will take the direct approach used in other fields and boutique and concierge medical practices. Straight-to-consumer marketing about medical services, technologies and devices, divisions such as cancer centers, and hospital systems is so pervasive that it seems commonplace.

ENTERING THE RING

The airways, Internet, and print media are crammed with appeals for elective surgeries and cosmetic procedures. One FM radio station near Washington, DC, carried competing ads from three different Lasik surgeons on the same day.

Hospital systems advertise on television, on radio, in print media, and online. "Come into our heart center if you have a problem," says the warm voice in the background of a TV commercial as actors stroll along a footpath in a meadow. "The people at XYZ Hospital were so skilled, I know I'm on the road to recovery," says the actor portraying a patient.

The accelerating trend in hospital TV ads is condition-specific targeting. Ads pinpoint patients in search of joint replacements, bypass surgery, liposuction, or tummy tucks.

Hospitals in Need

U.S. hospitals began advertising cautiously in the mid-1970s based on a combination of new government regulation and field guidelines and funding coming into the healthcare field. In the United Kingdom, hospitals could only engage in direct-to-consumer advertising starting in mid-2008, a generation after the phenomenon took root in the United States

Today, hospitals seek affluent, insured customers. Most ads about a hospital's services are designed to build brand awareness and create an image in the mind of the consumer. After all, how much can a viewer actually learn about a hospital or procedure from a 30- or 60-second spot? Not much, but good image advertising can successfully plant the idea that one hospital is better than the rest.

Hospitals also seek physicians who help draw patients to the facility. Often ad campaigns target doctors; such ads reveal that the hospital supports their programs. These ads serve to attract and retain quality physicians.

No Way Out

In the throes of the economic downturn of 2009, hospital advertising saw no decline, and in 2008, U.S. hospitals spent $1.23 billion on advertisements, slightly more than the $1.20 billion spent in 2007 but much more than the $493 million spent in 2001 (Newman 2009). As the cost of providing healthcare rises annually, competitive hospitals scramble for all the business they can get.

Nationally, in 2008 the typical small community hospital spent about $420,000 on advertising, compared to large teaching hospitals, which spent an average of $330,000, a figure that includes marketing, public relations, and community outreach.

The more hospitals in an area, the more fierce the competition. Having the latest medical equipment is a benefit to consumers, but if everyone has it and the equipment is underutilized, it doesn't pay for itself. So hospitals advertise, hoping to eradicate the unused capacity.

Unhealthy Partnerships

Hospitals that compete for business are not likely to collaborate. Thus, advertising competition can quickly get intense. A study by the Columbia School of Journalism concluded that some TV stations and newspapers end up forming "unhealthy alliances" with individual hospitals (Lieberman 2007).

In one case in Eau Claire, Wisconsin, a hospital partnership with a local TV station kept the station from doing business with any other rival hospitals in the region—potentially an actionable monopoly situation. After this arrangement became known, the TV station canceled the deal (Lieberman 2008).

THE RISE OF ADVOCACY JOURNALISM

More common than these media monopolies is advocacy journalism. With advocacy articles, a client hires a PR firm that writes about the client's operations, procedures, equipment, or products and services and attempts to persuade publications to run the article.

Some form of advocacy journalism has occurred in almost every profession in the United States. Publications often run the hospital-written features because they are generally well written and informative, and they publication doesn't have to pay for them. Similarly, some TV stations run short "health news" segments provided by hospitals—they are usually reasonably well done and free.

Of course, the potential loser in such arrangements is the public. Most readers and viewers don't understand that the material is coming directly from a hospital, and not through the usual filter of a journalist.

The Association of Health Care Journalists and the Society of Professional Journalists issued a joint statement imploring local media to not engage in advocacy arrangements, commenting that "content produced by hospitals does not fulfill the duty of news organizations to provide the public with independent medical reporting" (AHCJ 2008).

Product Placement

When you watch a hospital-centered TV show like *House, Scrubs, Grey's Anatomy,* or *Private Practice,* you might notice the highly visible brand names on the medical equipment. The brands appear as a result of vigorous product placement efforts by vendors and the show's producers, who pursue up-front revenue opportunities.

As with advocacy journalism, product placement is a practice that hospital executives need to acknowledge and consider. Could your hospital appear on a medical show to raise awareness of your brand among consumers? Whether to participate is your decision. Longtime employees and those who adhere to traditional methods of marketing might be resistant to such marketing.

THE HIGHER ROAD

How can your hospital share its message in an effective, ethical, accurate, and cost-effective manner? Getting the word out about your services and offering quality patient education is best undertaken by licensed healthcare professionals who are qualified to provide accurate information. Transparency of your operating statistics, full disclosure, and balanced narratives must prevail.

Consider the case of three neighboring medical practices that offer Lasik treatment. The broad span of their direct marketing is similar among practices A, B, and C. However, practice C includes disclaimers, cites risks, urges prudence, and demonstrably has the welfare of the patient in mind.

The consumer who is privy to the marketing outreach of all three practices notices that A and B provide all positive information and no caveats. Practice C stands out because of its candidness. Which practice's operating procedure immediately strikes a chord with the targeted recipient?

Honesty Is the Best Policy

Larson and colleagues (2005) found that many top providers employ the same questionable advertising techniques as pharmaceutical companies do. These findings were based on a study of the 17 medical centers on *U.S. News and World Report*'s "America's Best Hospitals" list. Researchers reviewed 122 advertisements that promoted 21 different specific services and found that hospital ads often manipulated patients' fears and other emotions and sometimes concealed the risks of certain procedures. Larson and colleagues acknowledge the necessity of advertising but believe hospitals "must be more sensitive to the conflict of interest between public health and making money. They must make a substantial effort to improve the nature of the ads by presenting a fair balance of benefit and harm information and minimizing the promotion of services of unclear value."

To comply with American Hospital Association marketing and advertising guidelines, hospitals must disclose procedures' risk in advertisements, but in the ads studied these risks were often masked or minimized. Researchers concluded that many of the ads seemed to place the medical centers' financial interests before the best interests of the patients.

Implications for Your Hospital

Honesty starts with your own public relations or communications department. All the information your public relations office gives out—online content such as newsletters and fact sheets, and print materials for the media—must adhere to the same high ethical standard.

When your spokespeople talk to reporters and journalists, speak at conferences, participate in symposiums, and otherwise issue messages that will be documented, replayed, and archived, and when your top executives, administrators, and medical staff are interviewed, you have the opportunity to influence people who will become your patients. You can also gain customers through organized events, community outreach programs, exhibits at health fairs, and all other forums where you garner more visibility and recognition for the hospital.

The Public Relations Society of America's Health Academy, the Society for Healthcare Strategy and Market Development, the

American Hospital Association, the Healthcare Strategy Institute, and other associations and societies offer information about taking your message public.

FOUR STEPS TO STAND OUT

In *Redefining Health Care*, Porter and Teisberg (2006) cite new opportunities for hospital suppliers, recrafted here for hospitals who find themselves in an increasingly competitive world.

1. Compete on delivering unique value over the full cycle of care by devising marketing strategies around the creation of unique value for patients. What do you provide for patients that no one else in your targeted area offers? Highlight this, and you'll begin to stand out more easily. Focus on cycles of care rather than episodes. Don't merely sell an operation or procedure, but sell the full package of what your hospital has to offer—the patient support, the unique care, and the expected outcomes.

2. Demonstrate value based on careful study of long-term results. Use evidence to display your value compared to consumers' other alternatives. Saying that a procedure has a 97.2 percent success rate is more definitive than saying, "With our skilled surgeons, you're in the best of hands." Better yet, incorporate both kinds of messages into your appeal. Accent your longevity as well. If you can offer longer-term data, such as, "For five years running, we've ranked #1 in the Delaware Valley when it comes to cardiac care," you're offering a level of assurance unmatchable by others.

3. Devise marketing campaigns based on value, current data, and consumer support. Concentrate your message on the value your patients get—satisfaction, peace of mind, and effective recovery as a result of expert care. Talk directly *to* the consumer, not *at* the consumer. Use "you" language—*you* receive, *you* will benefit, *you* will experience ....

4. Accent your support services that add value. What else do you do that adds value but is rarely touted in your appeal? Are your rooms larger? Are your halls quieter? Is your visitor parking lot safer, better-lit, or more convenient? Take a walk through your facility with new eyes, and from left to right, floor to ceiling, document what you have to offer over competing providers and beyond what the typical consumer might expect.

NOVEL APPROACHES TO MARKETING

For years, major hospital marketing campaigns have consisted of various forms of bragging. Citation of rankings is giving way to human interest stories.

Raw Emotional Appeal

In a campaign for Akron Children's Hospital, created by the Marcus Thomas Agency of Cleveland, real-life drama prevails. In a notable television ad, a teenaged boy, Austin, bald from chemotherapy, tells the viewer, "I don't really see like how this happened, the whole cancer situation. . . . I'm going to beat it, no matter what. It's just a disease." The ad ran on nearly 20 network stations and cable channels throughout Ohio and was unscripted. The young man was asked to speak and the cameras rolled (Newman 2009).

The hospital itself is nearly invisible in the ad, cited only in subtitles to show where Austin is. At the spot's end, a simple message appears: "See Austin's story. Tell us yours. akronchildrens.tv."

Only a few years ago, an actor would have depicted a patient. Viewers are now so sophisticated that the real thing—a patient—is mandatory.

Instead of talking about a hospital's equipment, state-of-the-art technology, skilled doctors, and caring nurses, more ads focus on a real person with whom the target market can identify. Austin could remind target viewers—mothers, who make most healthcare decisions—of their own children, so the ad is engaging.

No Frills, Nothing Fancy

New York advertising firm DeVito/Verdi, which has done work for Mount Sinai Medical Center, Massachusetts General Hospital, and Abington Memorial Hospital (Pennsylvania), has a list of commandments for making an effective, patient-focused hospital ad. "No pictures of doctors, no smiling people, no fancy machinery, no overpromises about medical care, no complicated medical terminology: just truthful expressions of critical care and breakthroughs" (Newman 2009). Your hospital would be wise to follow these guidelines.

These miniature case studies aren't likely to become passé anytime soon—human interest stories are much more appealing and resonant than facts, figures, and simple logic.

Do these case studies present the truth? Are they ethical, or do they prey on our emotions? If the patient and the condition are real, if the hospital treated them effectively, and if the results are true, sharing the story does not equate to misinformation.

THEY'LL HELP YOU GET THE WORD OUT

Empowered Doctor (www.empowereddoctor.net) helps medical practices generate visibility through search engine optimization. While the service is currently geared toward medical practices, the potential for hospital use is intriguing. Empowered Doctor works by targeting specific terms and geographic locations that are relevant to a medical practice in order to develop new patient leads the practice would not have otherwise received.

Empowered Doctor's site explains, "It is crucial that patients looking for your services are able to find you. Our service is designed to get your practice visible on page one of search results related to the services you provide and the [geographic] area your practice pulls from."

The Empowered Doctor team has experience and training in promoting medical websites so that people using Google, Bing, Yahoo!, and Ask to search for health conditions or services will find Empowered Doctor's clients. The service works by developing mini-websites that have the potential to attract more visitors for the medical practice but do not replace the practice's existing website. Working with your staff, understanding the range of your procedures and services, and differentiating key characteristics of your services, Empowered Doctor helps to show prospective patients why it's in their best interest to get in touch with you.

Once you review and approve the mini-website they've developed, Empowered Doctor launches a campaign for you. They continue to hone your mini-website so it becomes progressively more visible in search results. Empowered Doctor reports that clients typically see increased rankings within 15 to 30 days of the mini-website's launch.

More services like Empowered Doctor are sure to spring up soon. Because the cost of even one print media ad is staggering, paying a Web or consulting firm to manage a marketing campaign for you, particularly if it generates identifiable leads, is an alternative way of competing that simply has to be considered.

Implications for Your Hospital

You have a website and a Web manager, and undoubtedly you've done a fair amount of tinkering with the site over the years. Perhaps it's time to reapproach your Web presence, to turn your site into a proactive business generator instead of a passive online billboard.

THE HOSPITAL MAGAZINE

Most major hospitals offer monthly, quarterly, or thrice-yearly hospital magazines. *Hopkins Medicine* comes out three times a year and is published for alumni, faculty, parents, and friends of the Johns Hopkins School of Medicine, and "brings readers face to face with people, issues, and events that shape one of the world's leading healthcare institutions" (*Hopkins Medicine* 2009).

The four-color, high-quality publication explores healthcare, science, and the lives of faculty and students through a compelling journalistic eye. Its impact and message reach much further than to its stated target readership.

Creating Contact

The publication emphasizes how to contact the featured doctors. Readers are given local, U.S., and international patient appointment service line phone numbers.

Physicians outside of the Hopkins community may call a special toll-free number that operates 24 hours a day, seven days a week. This line was created "in response to the growing needs of physicians to reach Hopkins physicians quickly" (*Hopkins Medicine* 2007). That line is a subtle marketing masterstroke: it says "Here we are, we know we're good, we know you need to get in touch with us, and we've made it easy for you."

LEVERAGING A SOLID REPUTATION

In addition to the magazine, Johns Hopkins Medicine has a long and distinguished record of effective marketing, advertising, and publicity campaigns, including its 2004 "Imagine" campaign that presented "the historic and celebrated institution as distinctively poised to make many of the next great advances in medical science and practice, and to bring them rapidly to patients" (Rodgers 2004). The campaign blended black-and-white footage of classic stars who died too soon with footage of contemporary life, asking "What if Lou Gehrig had played just a few more seasons? How much longer could we cheer? What if Louis Armstrong never suffered a heart attack? How much more could we dance? We're about to find out." The ads emphasize Johns Hopkins' leading-edge research and its transformational power over medicine.

Developed with a communications firm, the Imagine campaign was primarily aimed at opinion leaders and had presence in the *New York Times Magazine, Forbes, Face the Nation, Sunday Morning News with Charles Osgood,* and *Meet the Press.* Beyond traditional print and television advertising, the campaign also integrated PR opportunities, its website, a film, and public events.

Edward D. Miller, dean and CEO of Johns Hopkins Medicine, stated, "There is so much noise in the marketplace about research and clinical advances that what's distinctive about Hopkins is often unclear or unrecognized. This effort…is a way to communicate directly with patients who need us, and with those who want to help us bring advances already in the pipeline to patients more quickly" (Rodgers 2004).

Implications for Your Hospital

If messages from institutions like Johns Hopkins have trouble rising above the din, it spells trouble for everyone else. If everyone is whistling the same tune, it makes marketing sense to whistle another. What services, benefits, or features can you accent that are unique to your hospital? Never mind going head-to-head, promoting the same services as your competitors. What can you accent because you excel at supplying it?

LOSE NOW TO WIN LATER

In early 2008, Emory Healthcare in Atlanta began a radio campaign directed toward potential heart patients, offering a $150 CT scan. During the first three months of the campaign, nearly 2,300 people responded to the ads by calling Emory, and 75 percent of those callers made appointments (Hendrick 2008).

Along with the $150 CT scan, patients received a detailed health assessment, ten-year cardiovascular risk outlook, and a calculation of their vascular age. While a patient could have gotten the scan at Emory and more expensive follow-up procedures elsewhere, the goal was to keep people with Emory for all their care.

Getting patients in the door this way can create future business and offset the cost of larger procedures and charity care. The ads were expensive but created business. The ads paid off in a greater way—they raised awareness and saved lives.

Implications for Your Hospital

Even if the cost of advertisements outpaced the money that came in from the CT scans, Emory's model embodies a smart idea. How can you attract patients for a relatively inexpensive introductory procedure and gain their loyalty (and business) for any resulting follow-up?

It makes sense to feature procedures for which your community has a significant need. If you're surrounded by baby boomers, offering CT scans that potentially lead to heart procedures is a viable strategy.

PULL THEM IN

Pull marketing is a strategy to create demand for a product or service by appealing to one segment of the distribution channel that can influence another. For example, pharmaceutical companies address consumers directly, through advertising, to induce them to ask their doctors for a particular medication.

The pharmaceutical lobby knows that consumer influence has a dramatic impact on what physicians are willing to consider and prescribe.

A hospital engages in pull marketing when it advertises to adults about medical services for their aging parents or to spouses about conditions that afflict their partners. Pull marketing is particularly effective when it creates advocates who influence and make decisions for the end users.

Implications for Your Hospital

If you need to start a strong advertising campaign, coordinate your efforts for optimal gain:

- Reexamine the demographic and psychographic data for your target market. Who lives nearby, who is most likely to patronize your hospital, and who has the ability to pay?
- What array of procedures and services does this primary market need?
- What introductory offer can you advertise to attract the market?
- What services can you provide that lead to a robust health assessment that informs the patient, raises awareness, and increases the probability the patient will return for high-ticket procedures?
- What message will help you to stand out in the region?
- How can you keep the campaign consistent with the reputation, quality, and image of the hospital?
- What nearby advertising agencies have extensive experience with the healthcare field?

BACK TO SLEEP FOR SAFETY

Promoting public health and safety around an awareness month or week has long been a popular and effective way to market healthcare services.

In Davidson County, North Carolina, 82 babies died between 2004 and 2008, an alarming rate of 8.5 per 1000 live births (NC State Center for Health Statistics 2008). To raise awareness of infant health and sleep issues such as accidental strangulation, sudden infant death syndrome (SIDS), and the strangulation hazards of sharing a bed with an infant and of excess bedding, in 2009 the Thomasville Medical Center partnered with the North Carolina Healthy Start Foundation. The partners gave onesies to every infant born in the center in October, SIDS Awareness Month. Each onesie bore a clear and unmistakable message about sleep safety: "Stomach to play, back to sleep, for baby's safe sleep."

The Thomasville center received onesies from the Healthy Start Foundation. A fact sheet in Spanish and English accompanied the onesies, along with tips for safe sleep and other educational items. Through the statewide initiative, more than 6,000 babies went home with the onesies (*Lexington Dispatch* 2009).

A Multi-Party Approach

To promote the campaign, the North Carolina Healthy Start Foundation issued press releases, which made their way to local papers, TV news, radio stations, and a variety of health-related websites.

When an article about the campaign was posted on the website of the local newspaper the *Dispatch*, many readers left comments, indicating how much the campaign was appreciated.

No one loses with health and safety awareness campaigns. The foundation gets credit and recognition for supplying the onesies.

The hospital gets favorable publicity and exposure for distributing them. The information helps parents put their babies to bed safely.

Implications for Your Hospital

The opportunities for your hospital to take a similar awareness approach are nearly endless. It is well-known that February is American Heart Month; what else can you promote throughout the year?

Chase's Calendar of Events can apprise you of important dates. For a list of national health observances, visit www.healthfinder.gov/nho/nho.asp.

Decide which awareness month or weeks to participate in. Determine where to put your time and energy, what will best serve the local people, which media outlets can spread the word, and what benefits your organization will get.

OH, THEM BONES

Bone and Joint Hospital at St. Anthony in Oklahoma City recently launched an advertising campaign to promote awareness of MAKOplasty, a partial knee resurfacing procedure aided by robotic arm technology. As the first facility in Oklahoma to offer the technology, Bone and Joint had a clear advantage.

The advertising campaign involved a variety of traditional and social media sources. The print/text campaign included newspaper, magazine, Web, and billboard advertisements.

Video ads ran on television, the TV station's website, and Bone and Joint's YouTube channel (www.youtube.com/boneandjoint okc). The ads gave viewers specific graphic portrayals of how the technology works and how it benefits patients.

One TV spot begins with a tongue-in-cheek disclaimer parodying the beginning of graphic TV shows: "The following contains material which may be offensive to those suffering with knee pain. Viewer discretion is advised."

The ad shows people golfing, jogging, and doing yoga, all overlaid with comical squeaks and creaks coming from their knees, and asks, "Hurting? We can help." A brief animation of the procedure is shown, followed by the hospital's contact information.

WE ARE THE EXPERTS

In 2009 the University of California, San Francisco Medical Center, launched an online advertising campaign to generate awareness of their Helen Diller Family Comprehensive Cancer Center. A recognized leader in cancer research and care, the center had recently obtained the highest ranking in its category according to *U.S.News and World Report*. The goal of the campaign was to make prospective patients aware of the cancer center's expertise, expanded services, and new state-of-the-art equipment. The campaign ran for six weeks on the online *New York Times*.

UCSF had surpassed the cancer centers at UCLA and Stanford, and it saw that distinction as an opportunity to spread the word. An animated online ad used four basic statements to show USCF's expertise (UCSF 2009):

- This year 1.4 million people in the United States will develop cancer.
- Just 40 cancer centers are qualified to call themselves comprehensive.* *Designated by the National Cancer Institute
- And only 1 is ranked the best in California.* *As ranked by *U.S.News & World Report*
- Click here to learn why UCSF is among the top ten centers for cancer treatment in the country.

Site visitors could then click on a link to the medical center's website, which provides detailed information about their clinical services and resources.

See It Live on YouTube

Methodist University Hospital in Memphis filmed and posted on YouTube the removal of a malignant tumor that threatened to paralyze a patient. The webcast was designed as a promotional campaign with three goals: to educate patients, help recruit top physicians, and lure donors. More than 21,000 viewers watched a preview of the brain surgery on YouTube. The hospital also received requests for appointments.

With the sometimes prohibitive cost of advertising, hospitals continue to scramble to reach prospective targets. The social media efforts detailed in Chapter 8 are attractive alternatives to costly traditional advertising methods.

Implications for Your Hospital

What noteworthy happenings in your hospital can be featured in an ad to draw attention and gain customers?

- Has your hospital won any awards this month, quarter, or year?
- Has your ranking for any division or procedure increased?
- Have you acquired new equipment, leading-edge technology, or new resources?
- Have you expanded your care?
- Do you offer new service alternatives?
- Have you increased convenience for patients?
- Have new doctors or other medical specialists joined your staff?

- Are you participating in a partnership program, a community outreach program, or something else worth touting?
- What behind-the-scenes stories would favorably influence your target market?
- Are you actively finding such stories, highlighting them to your best advantage, and profiting from the exposure?

RESOURCES ABOUND

Many periodicals, blogs, and books can stimulate your thinking about how to reach prospective customers.

Periodicals

These publications feature developments in hospital and healthcare marketing:

- *Medical Economics*: paper and electronic; http://medicaleconomics.modernmedicine.com/about
- *Marketing Health Services*, published by the American Marketing Association: paper only; www.amaorders.com
- *Hospitals & Health Networks*, the flagship publication of the American Hospital Association: paper and electronic; www.hhnmag.com
- *Healthcare Advertising Review*: paper and electronic; www.hcmarketplace.com
- *Healthcare Marketing Report*: paper only; www.hmrpublicationsgroup.com/Healthcare_Marketing_Report/index.html
- *Marketing Healthcare Today*: paper only; http://mhtmagazine.com/

- *Healthcare Call Center Times*: paper only; www.hmrpublicationsgroup.com/Healthcare_Call_Center_Times/
- *Journal of Hospital Marketing & Public Relations*: paper and electronic; www.tandf.co.uk/journals/WHMP
- *HealthLeaders*: paper and electronic; www.healthleadersmedia.com/magazine.cfm

Blogs

These blogs offer timely and innovative hospital marketing tips and techniques:

- Walking the Path: http://blog.pathoftheblueeye.com
- The Healthcare Marketer: www.thehealthcaremarketer.wordpress.com
- Market Share: http://blogs.healthleadersmedia.com/marketshare
- Hospital Impact: www.hospitalimpact.org
- Christina's Considerations: http://thielst.typepad.com/

These blogs also offer podcasts:

- Interval (a healthcare marketing and advertising firm): www.thinkinterval.com
- Marketing Edge Blog and Podcast: www.providentpartners.net/blog
- Hospital Marketing Journal: www.hospitalmarketing.blogs.com

Books

Several excellent recent books focus on hospital or healthcare marketing. One major text is *Hospital Campaigns at Work*, published by HealthLeaders Media. The 2009 edition features the winners of the previous year's HealthLeaders Media Marketing Awards. It's a valuable tool for a hospital marketer because it highlights creative in-house strategies you may be able to undertake without going to ultra-expensive advertising agencies.

These books also offer insight into hospital marketing:

- *The Complete Guide to Hospital Marketing*, second edition, by Patrick Buckley (HCPro, Inc., 2009)
- *Marketing Health Services*, second edition, by Richard Thomas (Health Administration Press, 2009)
- *A Marketer's Guide to Measuring ROI: Tools to Track the Returns from Healthcare Marketing Efforts* by David Marlowe (HCPro, Inc., 2007)
- *Healthcare Marketing Plans That Work* by David Marlowe (Society for Healthcare Strategy and Market Development of the American Hospital Association, 1999)
- *The New Rules of Healthcare Marketing: 23 Strategies for Success* by Arthur Sturm (Health Administration Press, 1998)
- *Healthcare Marketing in Transition: Practical Answers to Pressing Questions* by Terrence J. Rynne (McGraw-Hill, 1995)

These specialized volumes offer strategies for this era of intense competition and consumer-driven healthcare:

- *A Marketer's Guide to HIPAA: Resources for Creating Effective and Compliant Marketing* by Kate Borten (HCPro, Inc., 2006)
- *If Disney Ran Your Hospital: 9½ Things You Would Do Differently* by Fred Lee (Second River Healthcare Press, 2004)
- *Creating Consumer Loyalty in Healthcare* by R. Scott MacStravic (Health Administration Press, 1999)

- *Managing Patient Expectations: The Art of Finding and Keeping Loyal Patients* by Susan Keane Baker (Jossey-Bass, 1998)

Walt Bogdanich's *A Great White Lie: How America's Hospitals Betray Our Trust and Endanger Our Lives* (Simon & Schuster, 1991) is a studiously prepared exposé about hospital quality. While it's not a marketing book, it will give you insights on increasing quality for marketing purposes.

HOT TIPS AND INSIGHTS

- Taboos about hospital marketing and advertising to patients have fallen by the wayside; nearly anything goes.
- Often hospital marketing is used to placate staff physicians and to attract and recruit new ones.
- In an era when most hospitals aggrandize their service offerings, honesty is the best policy when marketing your services.
- Accent your strengths and position your hospital as the expert provider.
- Resources on effective hospital marketing abound and will stimulate your thinking.

CHAPTER 10

Converting Patients to Customers

IN THIS CHAPTER:

- The customer is king
- What is good customer service?
- To serve them, know them
- Customer relations management

HAVE YOU EVER SAT in a hospital waiting room for too long, feeling undervalued and underappreciated? For all the advances made in healthcare in the last decade, customer service still lags. While doctors today are more personable and engaging and some nurses and technicians have followed suit, as a field much work remains. Nothing short of a cultural realignment will do to make a hospital customer-oriented.

Throughout this book, the terms *patients*, *clients*, and *customers* have been used interchangeably, and we have frequently referred to the importance of treating patients like customers. Hospitals need to take a customer-focused approach to patients and prospective patients and embrace customer relations management tools and techniques.

Consumers are highly attuned to the level of service in healthcare. One in four customers surveyed has switched or has considered switching hospitals, clinics, or doctors because of a negative customer service experience. Slightly more than half of customers report that they chose a hospital whose employees seem to understand their needs. One in four customers has considered or patronized retail medical practices, walk-in centers, and concierge services to avoid hospitals and traditional medical practices (Entel, Huttner, and Machida 2008).

CHANCES TO BE CUSTOMER-CENTRIC

Opportunities to be customer-centered exist everywhere in your hospital. The quality of your staff members' interaction with customers makes a dramatic impact. Do your receptionists greet people enthusiastically, with sincere appreciation for their business? Or is the next person in the door simply the next person in the door?

Does every person who communicates directly with customers use warm, friendly, nurturing language? Or is the employee in a hurry, regarding the call as a distraction to her "real work"? Does your employee strand callers on hold, or does she treat callers the way she'd like to be treated?

Perhaps staff members are necessarily brief with customers, because efficient operations demand it. What doctor has time to sit and explain in everyday language the array of possible remedies? What nurse on a busy floor has the time to double the length of conversations to ensure that the caller feels satisfied and appreciated?

In today's ultra-competitive arena, each employee has to devote time to consumers, because there is no more efficient way to market a hospital than to adopt a customer focus and treat the customer as king.

As anyone in sales and marketing has learned, it is easier to do more business with existing customers than it is to find new customers. A business will be more profitable offering its services to a loyal base of long-term customers than it will casting a wide net and continually seeking the next new customer.

TALES OF CUSTOMER NURTURING

The fundamentals of keeping customers happy and ensuring their return are not mysterious. Take the case of Phil, a Good Insurance member who patronizes a small medical clinic affiliated with a large university medical center. When Phil arrives for an appointment, he hands in his Good Insurance card so that he is properly logged in. He then sits in the waiting room, but for no more than three minutes on average.

A nurse soon comes through the door, calls Phil's name, and leads him down the hall where he has a routine blood test, blood pressure check, and height and weight measurement. Then Phil sits in an office and briefly waits for Dr. Hiller, a knowledgeable, intense but friendly physician who arrives, on average, within six minutes.

Phil discusses his condition, often bringing a printed list of his symptoms and how he's tried to alleviate them. He knows from experience that Dr. Hiller appreciates the list, quickly reads it, and understands it. Dr. Hiller puts the list into Phil's hard copy file, then turns her attention back to Phil. Now Dr. Hiller works her customer-focus magic. She'll look with a physician's eyes at Phil's symptoms and offer Phil a variety of explanations for his condition.

"Let's Tackle This Together"

Dr. Hiller doesn't feel threatened by having Phil look up answers on the Internet, and she routinely provides guidelines for doing so. She'll tell Phil what to search for online, offering precise medical terminology. Dr. Hiller is open about the range of potential causes and treatments.

Prior to seeing Dr. Hiller, Phil consistently had a different kind of experience. His old doctors would examine him, declare a diagnosis with little explanation and no room for discussion, write a prescription, and say, "See me in a week." The old physicians would get upset if he challenged them or asked too many questions.

The first time Dr. Hiller ever suggested that Phil take the reins and do his own home-based research, it blew Phil away. He hadn't encountered a doctor like this before. Dr. Hiller is not ego-threatened. She's a participative physician.

Physicians who practice consumer-centered healthcare know the importance of involving knowledgeable patients in the process of becoming and staying healthy. Such doctors act like consultants to their better-educated customers. They realize that the customer might arrive with a wealth of information and already be armed with two or three viable treatment options.

"I Know Me Best"

No patient is likely to rival a physician for sheer knowledge of human physiology and medical science. Depending on the problem and the extent of his research, a patient could be somewhat on par with his physician for a particular issue. The interaction between patient and doctor is never a competition. Because it is the patient who is experiencing the symptoms, he has the best vantage point for reporting how he feels.

In essence, the patient arrives as a black box for the physician to observe and diagnose. The physician might have treated 20 others with the condition, but each customer has his own physiology with numerous factors that make him unique.

The customer-centered physician understands that today, offering options rather than a single, narrow prescription creates a highly different dynamic than that offered by a physician stuck in the age-old mind-set, "I am the omnipotent doctor; you are the meager patient." The customer who encounters a progressive doctor quickly senses a new kind of relationship, increasingly the only kind that educated customers will maintain.

ONE SIZE DOES NOT FIT ALL

Will a participative relationship work with all physicians and customers? No. Some customers want to remain as traditional patients and to be told exactly what to do. They do not wish to take their healthcare into their own hands.

Is there a generational effect among customers? Perhaps. Legions of younger customers who have never experienced the traditional doctor–patient relationship are more prone to arrive like Phil, armed with a reasonable amount of knowledge regarding their condition and possible remedies.

Is there a generational effect for hospital staff, starting with physicians? It's likely. The longer a doctor has upheld the traditional doctor–patient relationship, the harder it may be to convert to a more customer-focused, participative mode. This is not to imply that veteran physicians can't adjust; many have already made the conversion. They are well aware of the effects of the Internet, have witnessed shifts in customer behavior, and know that the people who patronize them are sophisticated.

Implications for Your Hospital

The larger your hospital, the harder converting to customer-centricity could be. Can you stratify your medical team by age or preference? Perhaps one group could continue the traditional doctor–patient relationship and everyone else could practice consultative medicine.

USE DATA TO SERVE CUSTOMERS

Suppose your hospital or healthcare system owns or is affiliated with a fitness or health and wellness center. When a patron swipes her card at the front desk, a world of opportunities awaits to support the customer focus, cement the relationship, and keep her coming back again and again.

What does your front-desk attendant do when a member swipes her card? Does he sit there, reading his magazine, barely saying a word to the member? The customer-focused organization employs information technology to gain profit and to offer the personal touch that enhances business. A customer-focused desk attendant does everything within reason to enhance the club member's experience.

On the log-in screen, the attendant quickly sees whether the customer is a board member, or has donated to the hospital foundation, or has a daughter who gave birth in the hospital last week, and can make a friendly comment accordingly. Maybe the health club member is on only her second visit. If so, the attendant should offer helpful insight: where the sauna is, how to find the extra towels.

Customer Focus Everywhere

Extend the example throughout the hospital to the physicians' offices, the rehabilitation center, the gift shop, your retail medicine stores or concierge services, and everywhere in between. All parts of the system operating in harmony let the customer know that he is king. Is this customer going to be loyal? Will he return repeatedly? Will he bring family, tell friends, and be among your most ardent supporters?

Too many hospital professionals misunderstand quality, thinking only about effective medical procedures and everything that supports them. How do you meet a customer's emotional needs in addition to his physical needs? That is what quality means to most customers. Hospital executives often have little clue that quality is defined by the customer, not by the provider of medical services. Even among enlightened hospital executives, great resistance to customer-centricity remains.

Implications for Your Hospital

How can you redefine quality care and customer focus at your hospital? What can you do to upgrade customer relations? The big task of becoming customer focused can start with tiny steps. From when a patient first calls your hospital to the time he is discharged, countless opportunities for providing customer service exist.

- How skilled are the people who answer your phones? They make the first impression.
- How user-friendly is your online registration form?
- How effortlessly can a first-time visitor navigate your website, gain answers to questions, and get real-time instant messaging or phone service if needed?

TO SERVE THEM, YOU MUST KNOW THEM

Can you determine which customers want to remain traditional patients and which are anything but traditional? Yes, and it starts with the information you gather from customers on the first encounter. You collect such data on the patient application form, and you also can train your liaisons—receptionists, administrative staff, and nurses—to subtly probe and determine whether a first-time customer is traditional or progressive.

Implications for Your Hospital

It is crucial to assemble a customer's clinical history to competently manage his health conditions. It is also important to acknowledge a customer as a person throughout his continuum of care.

- Where does he work; what does he do?
- Is he married; does he have children?
- What are his interests?
- What are his concerns?

Customer Relationship Management 101

Businessman and author Harvey Mackay observes, "Armed with the right knowledge, you can outsell, outmanage, outmotivate, and outnegotiate your competition" (Mackay 2010). To gain that knowledge about his customers, he developed the Mackay 66 customer profile, a roster of 66 biographical points used to gain critical information about each customer and prospect (www .harveymackay.com/pdfs/mackay66.pdf). The Mackay 66 is a customer relationship management primer.

To guide his sales force in developing a bond with customers and prospects, Mackay requires each of his employees to use the

Mackay 66. He has found that when his sales staff fills in most of the 66 profile points for each customer, they are better able meet customer needs, sell effectively, and build the company.

Mackay urges his employees to collect information from receptionists, staff assistants, and the customers themselves, and from suppliers, newspapers, and trade publications. He also implores his staff to constantly look for personal and professional information about the customer.

A Passion for Information Collection

Following the collection of basic contact information, the Mackay 66 asks for the customer's birth date, hometown, approximate height and weight, high school and college education details, college honors, degrees, college fraternity or sorority, college sports played—and that only takes us through item number nine.

Also among the Mackay 66 are military service; spouse's name, occupation, education, and interests; children's names, ages, schools, and interests; previous employment; offices held or honors; special interests; clubs; community activity; lifestyle; current health condition; favorite foods; sports interests; vacation spots; long-range personal objective; key business problems; and much more. The lesson for providers is clear: the more you know about your customers, the higher your revenues can climb.

LEARNING FROM OTHER FIELDS

Anecdotes from other industries help illustrate the fundamentals of customer focus.

Wine brokers are consumer-centric. If you enjoy fine wines, entertain often, and continuously seek new high-quality wines your guests will enjoy, a wine broker makes your life easier. Your broker calls every so often to tell you that he just bought a cabernet or that a new shipment of zinfandel will be arriving. You don't have to seek contact with the broker, because the broker reaches out to you. The broker, using customer relations management, calls all his clients periodically to keep them apprised.

Suppose you pull your car into an auto repair shop you haven't patronized before. Your car goes up on the lift, and soon you receive a diagnosis of what your car needs. Next comes the part you weren't expecting. In addition to offering the service that your car needs, the shop plugs your engine into their diagnostic computer equipment, then prints a roster of the current health of your car's engine—what services you're likely to need in 6 months, 12 months, and beyond. They offer the information as a free service without pressuring you to pay for things you don't need. You didn't know this report was coming and you didn't ask for it, but you are impressed. Even if you follow your car manual's suggested maintenance schedule, it's still impressive when an auto repair shop takes a proactive approach. When you need to have your tires inflated, you head back to the new shop. They do it without making you wait and don't charge for it. When your car needs anything else, you're going to return to that shop.

Dentists treat patients like customers, in part because the U.S. healthcare reimbursement system, which is based on mechanisms focused on prevention and long-term care, enables them to do so. Your dentist will tell you what teeth to watch and what future care may be needed. Your dentist is proactive and focused on what's best for you.

A Permanent Change

Hospitals can take lessons from everyone in business who takes a proactive approach to serving their customers, whether it's calling regularly, making suggestions, maintaining a database, or developing care schedules. Some service providers do their job so well that customers who move 20 or 30 miles away remain loyal.

Customer relations management is not a one-time event. Nor is it a management "flavor of the month" approach to treating your patients in an attempt to get more business. Customer relations management is an all-out, comprehensive approach to dealing with patients. In today's globally ultracompetitive environment, nothing less will do.

Your customers and prospects patronize a variety of other service providers and product vendors—health spas, boutique eye doctors, airport gold key clubs. Customers know which businesses get service right. When a nearby hospital provides better customer service than you do, it's only a matter of time before your competition gets the loyal, long-term, lucrative customers.

AUTOMATED CUSTOMER RELATIONSHIP MANAGEMENT SOLUTIONS

Hospitals run on information. They generate gargantuan amounts of it every day. In the new era of transparency, hospitals must harness information to continually improve performance and measure their record against competitors.

Customer relationship management (CRM) is the processes a company uses to handle its contact with its customers. CRM systems harness technology to pull together real-time data about a customer to allow you to better serve her.

Use of CRM systems in hospitals is growing, and for good reason. Simultaneously attempting to compete for lucrative customers, control costs, improve profitability, meet the demands of consumer-driven healthcare, deal with managed care, and foster a customer-focused culture compels hospitals to adopt systems and technologies that streamline operations. CRM systems can help your organizations excel in this manner.

Hospital executives use CRM systems to reduce and alleviate medical errors and their impact on patients, families, and the community. CRM systems that integrate clinical information with personal medical history have a direct impact on medical services' quality and providers' capability to avoid errors.

Hospital CRM systems offer integrated patient records that track and ultimately improve check-in procedures, customer care and recovery, and billing. Some CRM software provides integrated business systems that serve the medical staff, the administrative staff, and the hospital stakeholders. CRM systems also directly serve customers who seek easy access to their healthcare history and on-demand knowledge of their potential treatments.

Most effective CRM systems integrate personal health records with the hospital's data to provide a system for managing care-related activities, costs, and benefits while giving patients better access to manage their own healthcare online. Vendors generally offer demo versions of their systems so you can experience how CRM software can be applied in your hospital.

There are challenges to implementing CRM systems; they need to incorporate security safeguards, including patient confidentiality and privacy issues, HIPAA compliance, and system compliance. The systems can be costly, and employees may resist the change.

CRM System Vendors

Siebel Systems (www.siebel.com) is the early leader in CRM solutions for healthcare providers. Its healthcare package has been expertly tailored for the needs of providers of all sizes. This system is designed to help organizations to differentiate themselves from the competition.

Many hospitals use Salesforce (www.salesforce.com) as their primary CRM tool. The system is cloud-based, not software-based, and facilitates the collection of patient-related information from a consumer perspective, not a medical perspective. Viewing a patient's record shows which physicians have treated him; other labs, clinics, and specialists he has seen; and current and past medications. Nonmedical data may include family members treated at the hospital, whether or not the patient is a foundation donor, and whether she is covered by traditional insurance or self pay. Such data helps providers better manage and serve customers, particularly in offering them other helpful services and products.

HealthForce (www.healthforceonline.com) offers on-demand CRM applications for healthcare providers. The HealthForce system can be applied to intake processing, patient care, outpatient services, billing services, document management, and work flow automation.

SalesBoom (www.salesboom.com) offers on-demand CRM. Its basic components include salesforce automation, customer service, analytics, collaboration, and marketing automation.

EXPERT OPINIONS ON BECOMING CONSUMER-CENTRIC

At the "Leading the Customer Experience Journey" panel during Forrester Research's June 2009 Customer Experience Forum, three panelists, all responsible for their organizations' customer experience, detailed their consumer-centric efforts. Participants were M. Bridget Duffy, then chief experience officer at Cleveland Clinic; Aisling Hassell, vice president, customer experience and online, at Symantec; and Ingrid Lindberg, CIGNA's customer experience officer.

Duffy said that though it was her responsibility alone to transform the patient experience, she needed the full support of the CEO to do it. Lindberg and Hassell concurred that support from the top is vital. If your executive committee, department heads, and board of directors do not believe patients are customers and customers are king, no real movement toward consumer-centricity can happen in your hospital.

The panelists agreed that the task of changing to a customer focus was not simple. They warned to expect a solid year of frustration before changes become apparent. Some of the most encouraging movement was seen among physicians; they started out as the biggest obstacle, but most were able to adopt the new mind-set (Musico 2009).

Words Matter

CIGNA's Words We Use list is a commendable effort to improve the patient experience. The philosophy centers on health literacy, using simple, clear words patients can understand. Instead of saying "your liability," CIGNA says "the amount you need to pay." "Formulary" is changed to "drug list." More examples are available at http://newsroom.cigna.com/images/56/Words We Use.pdf. The language helps customers understand and trust the organization, and this relationship can lead to better health as patients are empowered and become active participants in their own healthcare.

Suppose for the first time you receive a bill with no medicalese. In plain language, line items simply state what each charge is for, in language you can understand: "blood draw," not "venipuncture." Receiving medical bills in English that explain how and why you're being charged is not just novel—it can be exhilarating. To know that your provider recognizes how important it is for you to understand what's going on makes all the difference in the world.

Fifty percent of healthcare consumers surveyed were interested in talking to a patient representative who would help them understand charges and bills, a strong indication of the potential marketing appeal of language simplification (Deloitte 2008). What would life be like if law firms, insurance agencies, airlines, and utility companies started using everyday language over the phone, in corporate literature, in their invoices, everywhere? You would have a newfound sense of personal control in dealing with those vendors.

Why the obscurity and arcane language? Language is power; the fine print is a form of repression. The airlines know you're not going to read the seven-page fine-print explanation of the terms of your plane ticket. You will buy the ticket and be glad to have a seat.

One reason for Southwest Airlines' profitability is that the airline has simplified transactions for its customers, acting straightforward and transparent, unlike its competitors.

Incentivize for Customer-Centric Care

Enacting change can seem impossible—even after countless seminars, memos, and reminders about the importance of customer service, some hospital employees still have negative attitudes, and old-fashioned routines and indifferences prevail.

How can you make your physicians care about customer experience? Grade them on it.

At Cleveland Clinic, every physician is on a one-year contract. They are graded on a scorecard, and that score is based in part on employee engagement and customer satisfaction. Happier customers mean a higher grade and better chance of renewal (Musico 2009).

Nonphysician employees in human resources, marketing, and information technology also may improve their customer service if they are graded on it. The accounting department staff and others who never physically encounter a patient can play a significant part in increasing customer satisfaction. Consider the way accounting departments traditionally prepare and distribute hospital bills after discharge. Who's to say that invoices cannot be customer-friendly?

Your Approximate Wait Time

Mercy Hospital in Miami offers an online ER wait time monitor (www.mercymiami.org/er-wait-times). Every 30 minutes, the site is updated with the number of people in the waiting area, the wait time to see a healthcare professional, and the wait time to see a physician. This useful service helps the customer feel like a king.

HOT TIPS AND INSIGHTS

- To convert from patient-oriented to customer-oriented requires a cultural reorientation.
- Quality is defined by the customer, not by the provider.
- Customer relations management is not a campaign or a one-time event, but rather an all-out approach for dealing with customers.
- Customer relations management programs are challenging to implement but worthwhile.
- Using simple language in all customer encounters, including your written materials and billing, can make a profound difference in the perceived quality of your services.

CHAPTER 11

Visions for the Future

IN THIS CHAPTER:

- Leadership in revolutionary times
- Customers have choices
- A near-term look
- IT spells the difference

YOUR HOSPITAL'S CUSTOMERS are its future kings and queens who will influence every aspect of your operations. Rather than become paralyzed by the notion that 10,000 years of streamlined medical dispensation is about to be turned on its head, realize that there is another way to proceed: recognize that with great tumult comes great opportunity.

FORWARD-THINKING LEADERSHIP REQUIRED

Consumer needs and demands will largely dictate which healthcare providers flourish. Effective, forward-thinking leadership is vital.

How can you support the consumer by becoming more transparent? Provide research data, meaningful comparisons, and up-to-the-minute information.

The role of information technology and the ubiquity of personal health records will streamline and make over operations, flow of information, availability of data, profitability, and, most important, quality of care. As consumer-driven health plans predominate in the marketplace, your patients' health plan choices serve as beacons that show which services to provide, which to highlight, and which to merely have available.

Preferences Count

Paying attention to consumers' preferences can lend an extraordinary competitive edge. Knowing that younger consumers embrace smartphone technology, social media, and multiple methods of gathering information—video, photo, audio, text, instant messages, and real-time conversation—serves as a blueprint for meeting the needs of this huge patient segment.

Understand the retail medicine phenomenon: the rise of convenience care, boutique medicine, and other variations that are likely to develop. Embracing this movement, rather than cringing at the thought of it, yields a panoply of new ideas and opportunities. Your hospital's longstanding reputation, brand, and specific services are the aces in your deck of medical care.

While the market for global and regional medical tourism continues to heat up, establishing service-line niches and promoting the benefits of staying home for care can secure your hospital's position. As with other developments in the quickly changing healthcare field, meeting the challenge of globalization head on is far more productive than throwing up your hands and lamenting, "What's the use?"

Customers Have Choices

With consumer-centric healthcare you need to bolster existing marketing to your consumers while establishing attractive, modern, ethical, appropriate, and compelling new ways to reach them.

Patients are truly becoming customers, and healthcare customers quickly learn that they have choices—most of the time, far too many choices. So when an outstanding local option appears, why wouldn't customers choose it?

A FIVE- TO SEVEN-YEAR OUTLOOK

Healthcare needs are not going to go away, but they are going to shift. Even with legislation and reform, expenses will increase because of healthcare costs, the ever-diminishing dollar, and increased consumer expectations. Efficient information and technology use will somewhat counterbalance costs, or at least slow their rise.

Providers adept at harnessing technology will prevail. As David Blumenthal, U.S. national coordinator of health information technology, remarks, "There's no way to transform the healthcare system without information technology" (Davis 2009). Likewise, there is no way to transform your hospital without information technology. Centralized data will enable coordination of care and improve reporting and billing.

Information technology will allow your hospital to proactively meet consumers' needs by coupling what you know about them with an understanding of the healthcare life cycle. Rather than responding in episodic fashion to singular healthcare needs, IT will allow you to take a holistic, systematic approach to customer care.

Supply and Demand

Insurance reforms make it likely that demand for high-quality healthcare will exceed supply. Provider supply constraints may cause delays in appointments, care, and follow-up visits. Accordingly, customers may feel as if appointments are being rationed.

A year after the state mandated health insurance, the number of Massachusetts adults who could not find a primary care provider increased 75 percent and waits for referrals rose to as long as 70 days (Long 2008). Such disturbance is an indicator of the potential disruption in supply.

With a decreasing ratio of primary care providers to customers, customer frustration is bound to boil over. This will fuel the growth of retail and boutique medicine, exacerbating the frustrations of hospital executives who bemoan the Walmartization of bread-and-butter services.

Years Before Profit

Acceleration of cost-cutting and reimbursement reform efforts will place continuing pressure on healthcare organizations to reduce waste, eliminate fraud, and reform billing and recovery practices (Battani and Zywiak 2009). Still, it will be years before such measures will make a notable impact on a hospital's profitability. The effects of new systems, procedures, and models of administration are hard to see in their early stages.

Consider the rise of the PC in the early 1990s: increases in worker productivity did not become apparent for almost a decade. Two decades later, the productivity gains are widely visible.

Hospitals' near-term profitability gains are likely to come from the elimination of misdirected efforts, redundancy, and waste. Doing more with less is likely to yield quicker, more discernable results than the implementation of systemwide measures will.

While no one can say precisely how healthcare reform's impact will unfold, it is safe to say that leaner, more efficient hospital systems will have strategic advantages in coping with the changes.

A PUBLIC HEALTH PARADOX

By approximately 2015, people 65 and older will account for nearly a fifth of the U.S. population (Battani and Zywiak 2009). This age group uses double the physician resources of those younger than 65. Accompanying this demographic shift is the onset of customers seeking care for chronic conditions. By some estimates, 70 percent of all doctor visits will be for treatments of chronic or recurring conditions, not just because of the aging population: health issues related to an overweight and obese population will continue to increase.

At the same time, the supply of general practitioners throughout the United States is holding steady, not increasing with the population. More doctors are specializing. Fewer see primary care as an attractive career choice. The availability of qualified nurses will continue to be a challenge. This may be offset by the immigration of doctors and nurses to the United States as the globalization of medicine prompts shifts in healthcare professionals' career decision making.

Active Adults and a Range of Consumers

More people than ever are maintaining highly active lifestyles far into their senior years, which will lead to unprecedented demand for related care. Knee and hip replacements and various orthopedic surgeries will see a marked increase before the decade is over, and they will increase exponentially in the decade thereafter.

Some consumers will take full charge of their personal health, aided by personal health records and information technology. At the other end of the spectrum, some consumers will continue to play a passive role, preferring to follow the old model where doctors are in complete command.

In the middle are healthcare consumers who will take charge of their health periodically, when prompted by illnesses, accidents, and personal wake-up calls. Some will dutifully come out for their annual checkup, flu shots, or whatever the issue of the day prompts them to do. Some consumers will haphazardly apply wellness measures as the spirit moves them or because they perceive it as an element of staying contemporary.

As the population ages, politicians, especially those representing older constituents, are likely to push for greater measures of governmental control of healthcare, despite pushback from more laissez-faire legislators.

TECHNOLOGY IS THE HOLY GRAIL

As IT improves, patient safety, security, and privacy issues loom large. Federal concern about patient privacy will prompt a new wave of regulation and compliance, adding to the cost of the widespread implementation of IT.

It is clear that hospital IT and the electronic health record will predominate. Yet over the next five to seven years, the picture is cloudy. Experts don't agree on how many healthcare organizations will have electronic health records in 2015; some predict 25 percent, others 75 percent (Battani and Zywiak 2009). A field that is only half technically advanced is a fragmented one. It makes no sense to come late to IT adoption, but the road to full integration is going to be rocky. It will be an odd sight: doctors still sporting pens and clipboards will walk the same halls as those who wouldn't think of proceeding without a smartphone, iPad, or other technological wonder.

Information technology will likely be the make-or-break factor separating competitive providers from those who merely hang on. IT makes all other field-wide developments possible, especially adoption of electronic and personal health records and implementation of consumer-centricity.

IT is the foundation upon which the future of healthcare and hospitals sits. The coming few years will prove to be a time of innovation and experimentation matched by frustration and exasperation, ultimately leading to transformation. Two steps forward, one step back, rather than uninterrupted progress, is likely to be the norm.

HOT TIPS AND INSIGHTS

- Forward-thinking leadership is vital to meet the challenges of consumer-centric healthcare; nothing less will do.
- Consumers' preferences are the blueprint for meeting their needs.
- It will be years before measures such as accelerated cost-cutting and operational reform make a notable impact on a hospital's profitability.
- The aging of the population and higher expectations of what healthcare can provide will profoundly influence the field.
- How you employ technology will be the make-or-break factor for your hospital in the coming decade.

Further Reading

Beyond the Gift Shop: Boost Revenue, Your Brand, and Patient Satisfaction with Strategic Healthcare Retail by Mindy Thompson-Banko (Health Administration Press, 2008)

The Complete Guide to Hospital Marketing, second edition, by Patrick Buckley (HCPro, Inc., 2009)

Creating Consumer Loyalty in Healthcare by R. Scott MacStravic (Health Administration Press, 1999)

A Great White Lie: How America's Hospitals Betray Our Trust and Endanger Our Lives by Walt Bogdanich (Simon & Schuster, 1991)

Healthcare Marketing in Transition: Practical Answers to Pressing Questions by Terrence J. Rynne (McGraw-Hill, 1995)

Healthcare Marketing Plans That Work by David Marlowe (Society for Healthcare Strategy and Market Development of the American Hospital Association, 1999)

Healthcare Tsunami: The Wave of Consumerism That Will Change U.S. Business by Dean Halverson and Wayne Glowac (Wave Marketing, LLC, 2008)

How to Swim with the Sharks Without Being Eaten Alive: Outsell, Outmanage, Out-motivate, and Outnegotiate Your Competition by Harvey Mackay (Ballantine Books, 1996)

If Disney Ran Your Hospital: 9½ Things You Would Do Differently by Fred Lee (Second River Healthcare Press, 2004)

Managing Patient Expectations: The Art of Finding and Keeping Loyal Patients by Susan Keane Baker (Jossey-Bass, 1998)

A Marketer's Guide to HIPAA: Resources for Creating Effective and Compliant Marketing by Kate Borten (HCPro, Inc., 2006)

A Marketer's Guide to Measuring ROI: Tools to Track the Returns from Healthcare Marketing Efforts by David Marlowe (HealthLeaders Media, 2007)

Marketing Health Services, second edition, by Richard Thomas (Health Administration Press, 2009)

The New Rules of Healthcare Marketing: 23 Strategies for Success by Arthur Sturm (Health Administration Press, 1998)

The Psychological Society: A Critical Analysis of Psychiatry, Psychotherapy, Psychoanalysis, and the Psychological Revolution by Martin Gross (Touchstone, 1979)

Redefining Health Care: Creating Value-Based Competition on Results by Michael Porter and Elizabeth Olmstead Teisberg (Harvard Business Press, 2006)

Websites of Note

Business Tools

Empowered Doctor (search engine optimization): www.empowereddoctor.net

HealthMedia (digital health coaching): www.healthmedia.com

HelloHealth (direct-pay practice setup): http://hellohealth.com

ZigBee Health Care (open standard for monitoring/management of healthcare devices): www.zigbee.org/healthcare

Customer Relations Management

HealthForce: www.healthforceonline.com

Patient Portal: www.patientportal.com

SalesBoom: www.salesboom.com

Salesforce: www.salesforce.com

Siebel: www.oracle.com/us/products/applications/siebel/index.html

Health Assessments and Decision Aids

23andMe (genome mapping): www.23andme.com

Dr. Greene—Pediatrics, Naturally: www.drgreene.com

Healthwise: www.healthwise.org

International Patient Decision Aids Standards Collaboration: www.ipdas.ohri.ca

My Family Health Portrait: https://familyhistory.hhs.gov

Patients Like Me: www.patientslikeme.com

WebMD Health Manager: https://healthmanager.webmd.com/manager

Health Videos

eMedTV: www.emedtv.com

HealthCentral: www.healthcentral.com

icyou: www.icyou.com

Marketing

Christina's Considerations: http://thielst.typepad.com/

Healthcare Marketer: www.thehealthcaremarketer.wordpress.com

Hospital Impact: www.hospitalimpact.org

Hospital Marketing Journal: www.hospitalmarketing.blogs.com

Interval: www.thinkinterval.com

Marketing Edge Blog and Podcast: www.providentpartners.net/blog

MarketShare: http://blogs.healthleadersmedia.com/marketshare

National Health Observances: www.healthfinder.gov/nho/nho.asp

Walking the Path: http://blog.pathoftheblueeye.com

Medical Tourism

BridgeHealth Medical: www.bridgehealthmedical.com

Healthbase: www.healthbase.com

HealthGlobe: www.myhealthglobe.com

Healthplace America: www.healthplaceamerica.com

Medical Tourism Corporation: www.medicaltourismco.com

Personal Health Records

Access My Records: www.accessmyrecords.com

Bartlett Personal Electronic Health Record: www.pehrtech.com

Datamonitor Group (assists with PHR currency and accuracy): www.datamonitor.com

Dossia: www.dossia.org

ER Card: www.er-card.com

Google Health: www.google.com/health

HealthVault: www.healthvault.com

Medicare's site about PHRs: www.medicare.gov/navigation/manage-your-health/ personal-health-records/personal-health-records-overview.aspx.

MedKey: www.medkey.com

My HealtheVet: www.myhealth.va.gov

My Health Info: http://health.msn.com/my-health-info-center

MyMediConnect: www.mymediconnect.net

myPHR: www.myphr.com

My Revolution: www.revolutionhealth.com/my-revolution

NoMoreClipboard: www.nomoreclipboard.com

Patient Fusion: www.patientfusion.com

Peoplechart: www.peoplechart.com

Practice Fusion: www.practicefusion.com

Trip Mate: www.tripmate.com

VitalKey: www.vitalkey.com

WebMD Health Record: www.webmd.com/phr

Telemedicine and Participatory Medicine

AeroClinic: www.theaeroclinic.com

American Telemedicine Association: www.americantelemed.org

Ask the Doctor: www.askthedoctor.com

Doctor George Says: www.doctorgeorge.com

MDLiveCare: www.mdlivecare.com

Society for Participatory Medicine: www.participatorymedicine.org

Society for Participatory Medicine's blog: http://e-patients.net

Society for Participatory Medicine's *Journal of Participatory Medicine*: www.jopm.org

Swift MD: www.swiftmd.com

Transparency

HealthGrades: www.healthgrades.com

Medicare's Hospital Compare: www.hospitalcompare.hhs.gov

References

Ad-ology Research. 2009. *Media Influence on Consumer Choice.* Westerville, OH: Ad-ology Research.

AMA-OMSS. 2007. *International Price Comparisons: Selected Surgeries.* [Online report; retrieved 8/5/10.] www.medretreat.com/templates/UserFiles/Documents/AMA Report June 2007.pdf.

America's Health Insurance Plans (AHIP). 2009. *January 2009 Census Shows 8 Million People Covered by HAS/High-Deductible Health Plans.* [Online report; retrieved 9/23/10.] www.ahipresearch.org/pdfs/2009hsacensus.pdf.

American Hospital Association (AHA). 2008. *Trendwatch Chartbook 2010.* [Online information; retrieved 9/24/10.] www.aha.org/aha/trendwatch/chartbook/2010/appendix4.pdf.

American Telemedicine Association (ATA). 2010. "What Is Telemedicine and Telehealth?" [Online information; retrieved 9/24/10.] www.americantelemed.org/files/public/abouttelemedicine/What_Is_Telemedicine.pdf.

Anand, G. 2009. "The Henry Ford of Heart Surgery." *Wall Street Journal* November 25, A16.

Association of Health Care Journalists (AHCJ). 2008. "Journalism Groups Warn Newsrooms Against Unhealthy Alliances with Hospitals." [Online article; retrieved 9/23/10.] www.healthjournalism.org/about-news-detail.php?id=59.

Battani, J., and W. Zywiak. 2009. "U.S. Healthcare in the Year 2015." [Online report; retrieved 9/23/10.] http://assets1.csc.com/health_services/downloads/CSC_US_Healthcare_in_the_Year_2015.pdf.

Beckley, E. T. 2003. "Visicu to the Rescue." *Modern Physician* 7 (3): 26.

Bennett, E. 2010. "Hospital Social Network List." [Online information; retrieved 8/28/10.] http://ebennett.org/hsnl.

Boodman, S. 2009. "Survey: AARP Magazine's Top Hospitals: If Your Diagnosis Is Serious, the Most Familiar Choice Isn't Always the Best." [*TODAY Health* online; revised 3/26/2009.] http://today.msnbc.msn.com/id/29899234.

Booz Allen Hamilton. 2007. "Healthcare Consumerism: Trends in Consumer Cost-Sharing." [Online document; retrieved 9/23/10.] www.boozallen.com/media/file/Trends_in_Consumer_Cost-Sharing.pdf.

Bothum, K. 2009. "Hospitals Embracing Social Media." [*The Delaware News Journal* online; published 11/10/09.] http://pqasb.pqarchiver.com/delawareonline/access/1897602111.html?FMT=ABS&date=Nov+10%2C+2009.

Chinai, R., and R. Goswami. 2007. "Medical Visas Mark Growth of Indian Medical Tourism." *Bulletin of the World Health Organization* 85 (3): 164–65.

Cleveland Clinic. 2010. "Overview." [Online information; retrieved 9/24/10.] www.clevelandclinic-jobs.com.

Consumer Reports. 2005. "Twelve Surgeries You May Be Better Off Without." [Consumer Reports Health.org article; retrieved 9/24/10.] www.consumerreports.org/health/free-highlights/manage-your-health/needless_surgeries.htm.

Dar Al Fouad Hospital. 2010. "About Us." [Online information; retrieved 8/5/10.] www.daralfouad.org/about.html.

Davis, B. 2009. "Transcript: Health Info Tech Coordinator David Blumenthal." [*Wall Street Journal* online; published 6/15/09.] http://online.wsj.com/article/SB124404155221081477.html.

Deloitte. 2008. "2008 Survey of Healthcare Consumers: Executive Summary." [Online report; retrieved 9/23/10.] www.deloitte.com/assets/Dcom-United-States/Local%20Assets/Documents/us_chs_ConsumerSurveyExecutiveSummary_200208.pdf.

DesRoches, C. M., E. G. Campbell, S. R. Rao, K. Donelan, T. G. Ferris, A. Jha, R. Kaushal, D. E. Levy, S. Rosenbaum, A. E. Shields, and D. Blumenthal. 2008. "Electronic Health Records in Ambulatory Care—A National Survey of Physicians." [*New England Journal of Medicine* online; published 6/18/08.] www.nejm.org/doi/pdf/10.1056/NEJMsa0802005.

Dolan, P. L. 2008. "Medical Travel Doesn't Have to Be Overseas." [*American Medical News* online; published 11/3/08]. www.ama-assn.org/amednews/2008/11/03/bisa1103.htm.

The Economist. 2008. "Importing Competition: The Coming Boom in Medical Travel Could Help Both Rich and Poor." *Economist*, August 14.

Entel, T., N. Huttner, and J. Machida. 2008. *The Empathy Engine: Achieving Break-throughs in Patient Service*. New York: Katzenbach Partners.

Epocrates. 2009. "Fourth Annual Future Physicians of America Survey." [Online information; retrieved 9/23/10.] www.epocrates.com/company/mediaroom/mediaresources/surveys/4th_FPAsurvey.pdf.

Ferguson, T., and the e-Patient Scholars Working Group. 2007. "e-Patients: How They Can Help Us Heal Health Care." [Online white paper; retrieved 9/23/10.] www.acor.org/e-patients/e-Patients_White_Paper.pdf.

Flegal, K. M., M. D. Carroll, C. L. Ogden, and L. R. Curtin. 2010. "Prevalence and Trends in Obesity Among U.S. Adults, 1999–2008." *Journal of the American Medical Association* 303 (3): 235–41.

Fox, S., and D. Fallows. 2003. *Internet Health Resources*. [Online report; retrieved 8/4/10.] www.pewinternet.org/Reports/2003/Internet-Health-Resources.aspx.

Fox, S., and S. Jones. 2009. *The Social Life of Health Information*. [Online report; retrieved 8/4/10.] www.pewinternet.org/Reports/2009/8-The-Social-Life-of-Health-Information/01-Summary-of-Findings/Summary-of-findings.aspx.

Gerfin, M., and M. Schellhorn. 2006. "Nonparametric Bounds on the Effect of Deductibles in Health Care Insurance on Doctors Visits—Swiss Evidence." *Health Economics* 15 (9): 1011–1020.

Gillentine, A. 2008. "Quality, Not Cost, Driving Increase in Domestic Medical Travel." *Colorado Springs Business Journal* October 31.

Goetz, T. 2010. *The Decision Tree: Taking Control of Your Health in the New Era of Personalized Medicine*. New York: Rodale.

Grohol, J. 2009. "About the Society." [Online information; published 6/28/09.] http://participatorymedicine.org/2009/about-the-society.

Halverson, D., and W. Glowac. 2008. *Healthcare Tsunami: The Wave of Consumer-ism That Will Change U.S. Business*. Madison, WI: Wave Marketing, LLC.

Harvard Medical School Dubai Center (HMSDC). 2007. "About HMSDC." [Online information; retrieved 9/24/10.] www.hmsdc.hms.harvard.edu/about_hmsdc.html.

Health Imaging News. 2008. "Primary Care Physician Drop-Off Cannot be Solved by Universal Coverage Alone." [*Health Imaging News* online; published 8/18/08.] www.healthimaging.com/index.php?option=com_articles&task=view&id=11837&division=hiit.

HealthGrades. 2009. *Sixth Annual HealthGrades Patient Safety in American Hospitals Study*. [Online report; retrieved 9/23/10.] www.healthgrades.com/media/dms/pdf/patientsafetyinamericanhospitalsstudy2009.pdf.

Hendrick, B. 2008. "Hospitals Advertise Services to Lure Patients Who Can Pay." [*Atlanta Journal-Constitution* online; published 4/7/08.] www.ajc.com/search/content/business/stories/2008/04/06/heartbiz0406.html.

Hobson, K. 2009. "Time to Switch to an Online Personal Health Record?" [*U.S.News & World Report* online article; retrieved 9/23/10.] http://health.usnews.com/health-news/articles/2009/09/16/switch-to-an-online-personal-health-record.html.

Hopkins Medicine. 2009. "Spring/Summer 2009 Home Page." [Online information; retrieved 8/5/10.] www.hopkinsmedicine.org/hmn/s09.

Hopkins Medicine. 2007. "About the Magazine." [Online information; retrieved 8/5/10.] www.hopkinsmedicine.org/hmn/hmm/about.cfm.

Horwitz, L. I., and E. H. Bradley. 2009. "Percentage of U.S. Emergency Department Patients Seen Within the Recommended Triage Time: 1997 to 2006." *Archives of Internal Medicine* 169 (20): 1857.

Huang, J. 2009. "Medical Tourism Proposal Sparks Innovations at Home." [Maine Public Broadcasting Network online; published 12/31/2009.] www.mpbn.net/Home/tabid/36/ctl/ViewItem/mid/3478/ItemId/10405/Default.aspx.

Intel. 2010. "The Next Step in Chronic Care Management: Personalized Health Monitoring at Home." [*Intel Health Guide* online; retrieved 9/24/10.] www.intel.com/about/companyinfo/healthcare/products/healthguide.htm.

International Patient Decision Aids Standards (IPDAS) Collaboration. 2009. "Home." [Online information; retrieved 9/23/10.] www.ipdas.ohri.ca.

Johns Hopkins. 2009. "About Us." [Online information; retrieved 9/24/10.] www.imc.jhmi.edu/aboutus.html.

Kent, C. 2007. *Marketing in Times of Price Transparency.* [Online report; retrieved 8/4/10.] www.cleverleyassociates.com/Library/Marketing.pdf.

Kent, C. 2006. "Marketing in Times of Price Transparency." [Online article; retrieved 8/4/10.] www.hospitalimpact.org/index.php/leadership/2006/ 10/26/marketing_in_times_of_price_transparency.

Kiplinger's. 2009. "Save on Surgery." *Kiplinger's Personal Finance* 63 (1) (January): 18.

Konschak, C., and B. Flareau. 2008. "New Frontiers in Home Telemonitoring." *Journal of Healthcare Information Management* 22 (3): 16–23.

Larson, R. J., L. M. Schwartz, S. Woloshin, and H. G. Welch. 2005. "Advertising by Academic Medical Centers." *Archives of Internal Medicine* 165 (6): 645–51.

Lexington Dispatch. 2009. "Hospital Will Promote SIDS Awareness in October." [Online article; published 9/28/09.] www.the-dispatch.com/article/20090928/ARTICLES/909284002?p=1&tc=pg.

Lieberman, T. 2007. "The Epidemic." *Columbia Journalism Review* March /April.

Lieberman, T. 2008. "Unhealthy Alliances Between Hospitals and TV Stations." [*Columbia Journalism Review* online; published 8/12/08.] www.cjr.org/the_observatory/unhealthy_alliances_between_ho.php.

Long, S. K. 2008. "On the Road to Universal Coverage: Impacts of Reform in Massachusetts at One Year." *Health Affairs* 27 (4): w270–84.

Mackay, H. 1996. *How to Swim with the Sharks Without Being Eaten Alive: Outsell, Outmanage, Outmotivate, and Outnegotiate Your Competition.* New York: Ballantine Books.

Medical Fitness Association. 2010. "Medical Fitness." [Online article; retrieved 9/23/10.] www.medicalfitness.org/displaycommon.cfm?an=1&subarticlenbr=250.

Medicare. 2010. "Learn More About Personal Health Records." [Online information; retrieved 9/23/10.] www.medicare.gov/navigation/manage-your-health/personal-health-records/learn-more-phr.aspx.

MedRetreat. 2010. "Frequently Asked Questions." [Online information; retrieved 9/24/10.] www.medretreat.com/medical_tourism/faq_s.html.

MSN. 2009. "MSN Introduces Online Tools to Help People Make Smarter Health and Lifestyle Decisions." [Online press release; retrieved 8/5/10.] www.microsoft.com/presspass/press/2009/oct09/10-01myhealthinfopr.mspx.

Musico, C. 2009. "Patients Are Customers, Not Case Numbers." [*CRM* magazine online, August 2009 edition; retrieved 9/23/10.] www.destinationcrm.com/Articles/Editorial/Magazine-Features/Patients-Are-Customers,-Not-Case-Numbers-55487.aspx.

NC State Center for Health Statistics. 2008. "2008 North Carolina Infant Mortality Report, Table 2." [Online report; retrieved 9/23/10.] www.schs.state.nc.us/SCHS/deaths/ims/2008/fiveyear.html.

Newman, A. A. 2009. "No Actors, Just Patients in Unvarnished Spots for Hospitals." *New York Times* (New York edition) May 4, B4.

Odiabat, H. 2010. "Malaysia Highlights its Strength in Healthcare, ICT and Green Technologies Among Other Service Clusters." [Online press release; retrieved 8/4/10.] www.ameinfo.com/229698.html.

Office of Public Health and Science (OPHS). 2009. "Surgeon General Declares Thanksgiving as 'Family Health History Day.'" [Online press release; retrieved 8/5/10.] www.hhs.gov/news/press/2009pres/11/20091125a.html.

Pew Internet and American Life Project. 2004. "November 2004 Activity Tracking Survey." [Online information; retrieved 9/23/10.] www.pewinternet.org/~/ media/ Files/Questionnaire/Old/PIP_Health_Nov04_Qs.pdf.

Porter, M., and E. O. Teisberg. 2006. *Redefining Healthcare*. Boston: Harvard Business Press.

Rand Compare. 2009. "Analysis of High Deductible Health Plans." [Online information; retrieved 9/23/10.] www.randcompare.org/analysis-of-options/ analysis-of-high-deductible-health-plans.

Rideout, V. J., U. G. Foehr, and D. F. Roberts. 2010. *Generation M²: Media in the Lives of 8- to 10-Year-Olds*. [Online information; retrieved 9/24/10.] www.kff.org/ entmedia/upload/8010.pdf.

Rodgers, J. 2004. "JHM Unveils a Marketing Campaign." *JHU Gazette* 34 (13): www.jhu.edu/~gazette/2004/29nov04/29market.html.

Sanders, E. 2007. "A New Source of Revenue for Hospitals, Clinics: Gift Shops Selling More than Flowers." *Business Journal of Milwaukee* November 30.

Sciamanna, C. N., M. A. Clark, T. K. Houston, and J. A. Diaz. 2002. "Unmet Needs of Primary Care Patients in Using the Internet for Health-Related Activities." *Journal of Medical Internet Research* 4 (3): e19.

Sensor, W. 2009. "Embracing Transparency." *Healthcare Executive* 24 (6): 50–52.

Seper, C. 2008. "Cleveland Clinic Won't Open a Branch in Shanghai." [Online article; published 4/24/08, revised 4/26/08.] http://blog.cleveland .com/medical/2008/04/cleveland_clinic_wont_open_a_b.html.

Shapiro, J. 2009. "Patients Turn to Online Community for Help Healing." [Online article; retrieved 8/5/10.] www.npr.org/templates/story/story.php?storyId =120381580.

Sharon, C. W. 2009. "Aon Consulting/ISCEBS Survey: CDH Plans Shift to HSAs." [Online report; retrieved 9/23/10.] www.aon.com/attachments/cdh_iscebs.pdf.

Swift MD. 2008. "Telemedicine is Good Medicine: On-Demand Healthcare Benefits Consumers, Employers and Providers." [Online white paper; retrieved 9/23/10.] www.swiftmd.com/xres/uploads/documents/SwiftMD-WhitePaper 20080819a.pdf.

Taylor, H. 2002. "Cyberchondriacs Continue to Grow in America." *Harris Interactive Health News* 2 (9): 1.

United States Department of the Treasury. 2009. "Fact Sheet: Dramatic Growth of Health Savings Accounts (HSAs)." [Online fact sheet; retrieved 9/23/10.] www .treas.gov/offices/public-affairs/hsa/pdf/fact-sheet-dramatic-growth.pdf.

University of California San Francisco (UCSF). 2009. "New Ad Campaign Promotes UCSF's Cancer Expertise." [Online article; published 6/1/09.] http://today.ucsf.edu/stories/new-ad-campaign-promotes-ucsfs-cancer-expertise.

Wallask, S. 2009. "Twitter Can Play Key Role in Disaster Management." [Health-Leaders Media online article; published 12/30/09.] www.healthleadersmedia.com/content/TEC-244259/Twitter-Can-Play-Key-Role-in-Disaster-Management.

Weissman, J. S., C. L. Annas, A. M. Epstein, E. C. Schneider, B. Clarridge, L. Kirle, C. Gatsonis, S. Feibelmann, and N. Ridley. 2005. "Error Reporting and Disclosure Systems: Views from Hospital Leaders." *Journal of the American Medical Association* 293 (11): 1359–66.

Wharam, J. F., B. E. Landon, A. A. Galbraith, K. P. Kleinman, S. B. Soumerai, and D. Ross-Degnan. 2007. "Emergency Department Use and Subsequent Hospitalizations Among Members of a High-Deductible Health Plan." *Journal of the American Medical Association* 297 (10) (March 14): 1093–1102.

Wilkinson, O. M., F. Duncan-Skingle, J. A. Pryor, and M. E. Hodson. 2008. "A Feasibility Study of Home Telemedicine for Patients with Cystic Fibrosis Awaiting Transplantation." *Journal of Telemedicine and Telecare* 14 (4): 182–85.

Wojcieszak, D., J. Banja, and C. Houk. 2006. "The Sorry Works! Coalition: Making the Case for Full Disclosure." *Joint Commission Journal on Quality and Patient Safety* 32 (6): 344–350.

Zuckerman, A. P. 2010. "Congressional Twitter Usage Results Are In!" [Online article; posted 6/16/10.] www.findingzuckerman.com/2010/06/congressional-twitter-usage-results-are.html.

Index

23andMe, 69, 201

AARP, 13
Access My Records, 60, 202
advertising. *See* marketing
AeroClinic, 203
Alegent Health, 16, 18, 86
    My Cost, 18
American Academy of Family Physicians' Center for Health Information Technology, 52
American Health Information Management Association, 60
American Hospital Association, 13
American Nurses Association, 13
American Telemedicine Association, 203
Aon Consulting, 73, 77–78
apps. *See under* smartphones
Arrow, Kenneth J., 7
Ask the Doctor, 109, 203
Association of Health Care Journalists, 156

Baker, Susan Keane, 199

Bartlett Personal Electronic Health Record, 60, 203
Berwick, Donald, 12
Beyond the Gift Shop, 99, 199
BlueCard network, 127
Blumenthal, David, 193
Bogdanich, Walt, 199
Booz Allen Hamilton, 80
Borten, Kate, 200
Bosworth, Adam, 58
boutique medicine. *See* concierge medicine
BrainTalk, 150
BridgeHealth Medical, 131–32, 202
Buckley, Patrick, 199

Cancer Therapeutics Research Group, 122
cell phones. *See* smartphones
Center for Democracy and Technology, 63
Centers for Medicare & Medicaid Services, 16
Christina's Considerations, 202
CIGNA, 188
Citysearch, 44

HSAs. *See under* consumer-driven
  health plans
Hulu. *See under* social media

icyou. *See under* social media
If Disney Ran Your Hospital, 199
information technology (IT), 27–45
  costs of, 28–29
  evaluation of, 41
  patient feedback collection, 44
Institute for Healthcare Improve-
  ment, 12
Intel Health Guide, 105
International Patient Decision Aids
  Standards Collaboration, 82, 202
International Society of Certified
  Employee Benefit Specialists, 73
Interval, 202
iPhone. *See* smartphones

Johns Hopkins Medicine, 122, 148
Johns Hopkins Singapore Interna-
  tional Medical Centre, 122
Journal of Participatory Medicine,
  40–41, 179
Journal of Telemedicine and Telecare, 106

Kassabgi, George, 58
Keas, 58. *See under* electronic PHR
  systems
Kent, Carolyn, 8, 10

Lake Nona Science and Technology
  Park, 127–28
lawsuits, 12
Lee, Fred, 199
LinkedIn. *See under* social media
Little Clinic, 96. *See also* retail
  medicine

Mackay, Harvey, 199
MacStravic, R. Scott, 199
Managing Patient Expectations, 199
Marketer's Guide to HIPAA, A, 200

*Marketer's Guide to Measuring ROI,
  A*, 200
marketing (direct to consumer),
  153–74
  advertising journalism, 156
  American Hospital Association
    compliance with, 158
  downside of, 155–56
  ethical standards of, 158–59
  hospital magazines, 163
  product placement, 156–57
  public health campaigns, 167–71
  pull marketing, 165–66
  resources for, 171–74, 202
  tips for, 159–61
Marketing Edge, 202
Marketing Health Services, 200
"Marketing in Times of Price Trans-
  parency," 8
MarketShare, 202
Marlowe, David, 199, 200
Mayo Clinic, 110, 125
MDLiveCare, 109, 203
Medical Tourism Association, 116
Medical Tourism Corporation
  (MTC), 117–18, 202
Medical Tourism Magazine, 116
Medical University of South Caro-
  lina, 148
Medicare, 13–14, 61
  PHR site for, 203
  transparency site for, 204
MedKey, 60, 203
Microsoft HealthVault. *See also* elec-
  tronic PHR systems
Miller, Edward D., 164
MinuteClinic, 58, 96. *See also* retail
  medicine
My Family Health Portrait, 48–49, 202
My Health Info, 203
My Health*e*Vet, 60, 203
My Revolution, 60, 203
MyMediConnect, 51, 59, 203
myPHR, 60, 203

About the Authors

Colin B. Konschak, MBA, FACHE, is the managing partner of DIVURGENT, a healthcare management consulting firm. During his 20 years in the healthcare sector, he has focused on helping healthcare providers understand the shifting healthcare/technology marketplace and plan their organizational and technology direction accordingly. Mr. Konschak has broad experience in healthcare operations, strategic planning, and health information technology. Mr. Konschak is a registered pharmacist, has an MBA in health services administration, is board certified in healthcare management, and is a certified Six Sigma Black Belt. He is currently an adjunct professor at Old Dominion University, leading classes on performance improvement, negotiation, and business ethics in their MBA program.

Lindsey P. Jarrell, MHA, FACHE, is the cofounder of Source88, a healthcare IT consulting firm. Mr. Jarrell is a highly accomplished healthcare executive with more than 15 years of experience and an exceptional record of achievement in consulting, clinical transformation, product advisory roles, strategic planning, contract negotiation, and CIO leadership in a large integrated delivery network. In 2009 Mr. Jarrell was recognized in the InformationWeek 500 List and the CIO 100 Winners and was awarded the CHIME-AHA 2009 Transformational Leadership Award. He serves as a coach and friend to many health system executives across the United States. Mr. Jarrell holds a master's and a bachelor's degree in health services administration.